MEET THE MAFIA

Joe Colombo, Sr., who almost convinced the world that the Mafia was a myth, before very real bullets gunned him down . . . Frank Sinatra, whose intimate connections with the Mafia have never before been fully revealed . . . Meyer Lansky, the financial czar who has expanded Mafia methods to include Swiss bank accounts and Harvard Business School techniques . . . the multitude of Mafia enterprises that range from drugs and numbers to Wall Street and Washington . . . the Mafia lifestyle, with its wives and mistresses, sons and daughters . . . the Mafia and the Black underworld . . . the leading Mafiosos throughout the country today . . .

This book takes you all the way inside the Mafia. It is compulsively fascinating and important reading.

"It communicates the real nature of organized crime today: its organization, its leaders, its rackets, its heroes and victims, its history and internal struggles. Anyone who reads it will come away not only entertained, but informed about the danger of the magnitude of the national crime network!" —ROBERT M. MORGENTHAU

THE MAFIA IS NOT AN EQUAL OPPORTUNITY EMPLOYER

NICHOLAS GAGE

Foreword by
ROBERT M. MORGENTHAU

A DELL BOOK

To my wife, Joan, and
my son, Christos

Published by
DELL PUBLISHING CO., INC.
750 Third Avenue
New York, New York 10017

The author makes grateful acknowledgment for
permission to reprint the following selections:
"Meyer Lansky—Underworld Genius"
Copyright © 1970 by The Atlantic Monthly
Company, Boston, Mass.
"Organized Crime in the Ghetto" and sections
of "Joe Colombo—Mafia Maverick" © 1970/1971
by the New York Times Company. Reprinted
by permission.
"Bias in the Mafia," "Organized Crime Abroad,"
and "High Rollers on High" reprinted by
permission from *The Wall Street Journal*.
"Organized Crime in the Supermarket"
reprinted by permission from the August, 1971
issue of *Good Housekeeping*. © 1971 by the
Hearst Corporation.

CONTENTS

FOREWORD

ORGANIZED CRIME in the United States has existed for several decades. Newspapers and magazines have consistently reported on its surface manifestations—the bloody wars between rival gangs and the flashy life styles of gang leaders. But only in recent years have Americans been given a profound look into the operations of organized crime and been made to see the menace that it represents to our society. Among the principal guides on these disturbing tours have been the men who practice a relatively new kind of journalism called investigative reporting.

During my nine years as United States Attorney for the Southern District of New York—years spent prosecuting thousands of criminal cases including more than 150 involving major organized crime figures—I came to know many of the best investigative reporters in the country. Among them is Nicholas Gage.

Top-flight investigative reporters like Nick prod busy and sometimes indifferent law enforcement officials to investigate and prosecute complicated organized crime cases that they might otherwise overlook. If there were more reporters with his skill and tenacity, the fight against organized crime in the United States would be more effective.

Nick Gage has written extensively about the internal workings of the mob for *The Wall Street Journal, The New York Times,* and a number of leading magazines. As the title of this book indicates, Nick often writes about the underworld with touches of wry humor. His lucid and colorful style leads the reader effortlessly through the welter of names, aliases, legal terms, and court decisions that often make thorough reports about organized crime difficult for the layman to understand.

This book, without ever being didactic, communicates the real nature of organized crime today: its organization, its leaders, its rackets, its heroes and victims, its history and internal struggles. Anyone who reads it will come away not only entertained, but much better informed about the danger and the magnitude of the national criminal network. And, along with Nicholas Gage, he will be well aware that organized crime, for all its color and drama, is no laughing matter.

Robert M. Morgenthau

INTRODUCTION

CONFESSIONS OF AN INVESTIGATIVE REPORTER

EVERYBODY KNOWS how a big-city newspaper covers crime news—we have seen it often enough on the late show. The hard-bitten city editor, talking out of the side of his mouth around his cigar, calls in our hero and shouts, "Awright, Rafferty, I want you to find out who murdered that girl and I want you to do it in time for the seven o'clock edition!" Rafferty, who is also tough but has the heart of a marshmallow, throws on his trench coat and his hat, all the while muttering curses upon the city editor. But he always gets his man in time for the deadline.

News of crime and corruption has been the backbone of journalism ever since Gutenberg invented movable type, but in the last ten years or so a new kind of crime reporter has appeared. His stories concern not the day-to-day police news but the machinations of organized crime and the behind-the-scenes corruption of politicians and public figures whose misdeeds could never be ferreted out between 10 A.M. and the 7 P.M. deadline.

Of course, there have always been such reporters and journalists; the muckrakers early in the century, exposing the evils of child labor, sweatshops, mistreatment of mine workers, unsanitary packaging of meats—these were the forerunners of today's investigative reporters. The difference is that the muckrakers frequently made themselves the heroes of their own stories and tended to sensationalize their facts. By contrast, investigative reporters let the facts speak for themselves.

Only within the last decade have the larger newspapers and magazines begun hiring individuals solely for the purpose of investigative reporting. The publications give these journalists the time, money, and freedom to report not what a district attorney tells them or the words of an indictment, but information that the reporter has dug up for himself—information that the reader would never find out otherwise.

As a result, a number of stories have come to light that would previously never have found a place on the front page between the political feuds and the rock festivals. And investigative reporters' stories in turn make their own news:

—The resignation of Supreme Court Justice Abe Fortas was a direct result of the work of William Lambert of *Life* magazine, who discovered that Fortas had accepted a $25,000 check from Louis Wolfson when Wolfson was under indictment for stock manipulations.

—A whole government fell in the Bahamas in 1966 after Stanley Penn of *The Wall Street Journal* reported that a number of the ruling party's leaders had accepted consultants' fees from land developers and casino operators.

—The world learned that American political leaders had been less than frank with Congress and the American people about Vietnam policy when *New York Times* reporter Neil Sheehan secured a secret Pentagon study of the history of that war.

—Articles by a number of investigative reporters made the public aware of the degree to which organized crime had infiltrated all levels of society and they brought about federal legislation broadening the weapons that law enforcement officials could use in fighting organized crime.

Journalists hired solely for the purpose of investigative reporting have produced so many dramatic stories and major headlines and have performed such a public service that many large papers and magazines have added investigative reporters to their staffs. But the degree of commitment and competence of both the publications and their investigative reporters varies greatly. Some publications allow a regular reporter to follow a story in depth now and then, relieving him from the pressure of the daily assignment. And occasionally there are good reporters who, sensing a major story, will doggedly pursue it even in the face of opposition from their editors. But there are really only about a dozen United States newspapers and magazines with a total commitment to investigative reporting.

Many editors understandably hesitate when it actually comes to authorizing tough investigative reporting. For one thing, it is very expensive. A reporter may fly all over the country and even to Europe chasing wispy rumors and leads that abruptly turn out to be dead ends. It has been estimated that *The New York Times,* for example, spent more than $100,000 for salaries, security measures, research, and related expenses before it broke the story of the Pentagon papers.

Furthermore, an investigation bears fruit only slowly. Bill Lambert spent more than six months on the Fortas story from the moment he got the first tip, cultivated possible sources, documented the evidence, and double-checked his information until the time he finally wrote the story.

And when a story is in print, the publication

may find itself not only with dramatic headlines, but also with a big, fat lawsuit. Even if a story is airtight and the reporter can prove it in court lawsuits are expensive. *Life* magazine has spent more money on legal fees to support its investigative reporting team than it has on actually financing the team.

One of the several questions commonly put to investigative reporters by acquaintances is, Where do you get your stories? Unlike Rafferty, who was sent out to find the murderer by 7 P.M., a real live investigative reporter does not spend a lot of time knocking on doors that are opened by beautiful blondes or peering through a telescope from behind the curtains of a rented room into the room across the street. Nor does an investigative reporter spend most of his time in bars with his hat pulled down over his eyes and his ears open. (On the other hand, I did once spend a long and wearying evening in a hotel bar cultivating the bartender while waiting to catch a certain public figure as he emerged with a female friend from a hotel suite frequently lent to him by a convicted criminal.)

The investigative reporter probably spends much less time in bars than he does shuffling through file drawers full of dusty legal papers in courthouse archives, or cooling his heels in the waiting rooms of men who do not want to talk to him.

Most important to an investigative reporter, ranking somewhere above his editor, newspaper, wife, and children, are his sources. All the great stories come to the reporter from someone who trusted him enough to show him or give him documents that prove wrongdoing on someone's part. Bill Lambert won the confidence of a man who had access to a copy of the check sent to Fortas. Neil Sheehan was not given access to the Pentagon papers because he had charmed some confidential secretary in the Defense Department, but because his previous articles on Vietnam had inspired confidence and respect in Daniel Ellsberg, who had access to the papers and the inclination to reveal them.

One of the first stories I did for *The New York Times* concerned a state supreme court judge who had long been rumored to be bending the canons of judicial ethics. Before my arrival, one of the *Times*'s competent reporters had spent many weeks trying to track down the rumors, but he was not able to accumulate enough facts to support a story. Luckily, sources I had acquired while working on previous investigative stories for *The Wall Street Journal* and other publications proved useful. Within a short time after being assigned the story, I managed to uncover solid evidence that the judge, contrary to judicial rules, had discussed cases with defense counsels outside the courtroom, that he had on several occasions met a notorious fixer, and that he had done favors for several convicts.

Understandably, the best investigative reporters will protect the identity of their sources above all else. "My first loyalty is to my source, then to my newspaper," says one Pulitzer Prize winner. "I can always find another job, but if I betray one source, I'm through."

Who are these sources and where do they come from? They may be law enforcement officials who can provide records not accessible to the public. They may be disgruntled employees, angry ex-wives, conscience-stricken public servants, jealous business or political rivals, or ordinary citizens who have lost confidence in seeing justice done by their local law enforcement authorities. They may contact a reporter, or the reporter may search them out, perhaps figuring that a notorious criminal's ex-wife is just about angry enough to tell a few secrets to a reporter if her identity is well protected. Like a lawyer, an investigative reporter must keep in mind that his sole responsibility is to determine the accuracy of the source's information, not to dig for the reason the source is giving it nor to be put off the scent by the source's sometimes unsavory reputation.

The question that every investigative reporter hears most often is, Aren't you afraid that one of these days one of the criminals you write about will decide to get even with you? Of course, there's always that possibility, and perhaps an investigative reporter does look over his shoulder more often than the average citizen does, but I do not know any investigative reporters who lose sleep worrying about gangland reprisals. Although gangsters occasionally have shot reporters in the past, I suspect that, deep down, many organized crime figures enjoy seeing their names in print. Once a gangster telephoned me at my office the morning after his name had figured in an article I had written. I acknowledged writing the article and braced myself for what was coming next. "Listen," he growled, "you spelled my name wrong. It starts with an S, not a C."

A reporter courts real danger only if he tries to develop a personal relationship with racketeers and accepts money or presents from them. When an organized crime figure feels that he has been betrayed, his vengeance will be swift and merciless. But in most cases underworld figures realize that if they turned violently against a reporter they would only reap still more publicity from other journalists—the very thing they were trying to avoid.

Another question often put to an investigative reporter is whether he uses disguises to get a story. While I have never donned a false mustache or posed as a telephone repairman, I have occasionally assumed a false identity. For one of my first investigative stories, I took a job as an attendant in a Massachusetts state school for retarded children, and the experience led to a series of articles that ultimately brought about reforms in the operation of the school. Another, more enjoyable ruse was posing as a wealthy Greek shipowner traveling to London on a junket with high-rolling United States gamblers (see Chapter 12). For a series of articles on the unfair practices of some employment agencies in Massachusetts, I posed as a whole series of characters from an engineer to an alcoholic parking attendant. The poses paid off in a number of articles that ultimately led to a Massachusetts law limiting the fees that agencies can charge.

In spite of such occasional gratifications, the life of an investigative reporter is hardly an enviable one. First, he has to dig into a story that a great many people usually want to hush up. Then, once he has his story, he has to convince his editors that it is worth printing.

It is pointless to pass judgment on the quality of investigative reporting in given publications because a paper or magazine is only as strong as its current editors. An investigative reporter with editors who will stand behind him is a happy man. It does not always turn out that way, however. Several years ago a Boston paper hired me and three other investigative reporters to form a "crack team" that would astonish the city by exposing crime and corruption of all kinds. Things went smoothly until two members of the team, Hank Messick and James Savage, began investigating the underworld ties of Joseph Linsey, a prominent Boston businessman. They were called into the office of the publisher and asked to drop that particular line of investigation. To investigative reporters this is like offering catnip to a cat. We soon discovered that Mr. Linsey was a stockholder in the newspaper that employed us. The upshot of the matter was that one of the reporters was fired, and the rest of us quit in protest. (The newspaper did not quite succeed in suppressing the story, however, and a number of other papers covered it.)

From Boston I had the good luck to go to *The Wall Street Journal* and later to *The New York Times,* and both New York papers provided the strong editorial support that makes the frustrations of investigative reporting easy to bear. But investigative reporters are not often so fortunate, and as a result they frequently hear themselves saying "I quit!" (and find their editors eagerly accepting their offer).

The career of Hank Messick, one of my colleagues in Boston, is a case in point. In the 1950's Hank was working for the Louisville *Courier-Journal* when he broke the story of how organized crime had turned nearby Newport, Kentucky, into a wide-open "sin city" supported by illegal gambling, prostitution, and every kind of graft.

At first Hank was applauded for his efforts, but after Newport was cleaned up, his continued emphasis on crime and corruption in other parts of Kentucky was seen as undermining the state's image, and his stories were received with rapidly declining enthusiasm.

He then moved to Miami, where, as an investigative reporter for the Miami *Herald,* he revealed that the city was full of powerful members of organized crime. Every now and then, in a column called "Know Your Neighbor," Hank would disclose the underworld past of one of the big investors in Miami Beach. But when he moved on to describe connections between well-known Miami businessmen and the underworld, things became a bit warm around the *Herald,* and his stories were run less and less often. So he quit, and a short time later he accepted the ill-fated job on the investigative team of the newspaper in Boston. From there Hank returned once again to Miami. He went to work for a small local paper called the Miami Beach *Sun,* where again he began digging into the important role organized crime plays in Miami's economy. After he had been there nearly a year, the *Sun* was sold to a new owner; the first man to receive his walking papers was Hank. On the same day, Hank received an unexpected telephone call from Ben Cohen, a Miami lawyer who represented a number of the men who had been raked over the coals in Hank's articles. "I hear you've been fired," the lawyer began, and when Hank said it was true, the lawyer snarled, "Well, I hope you rot in the gutter, you son of a bitch!"

Since then, Hank, forty-eight and the father of three, has supported himself and his family by writing books about organized crime, specializing in the non-Mafia side of the mob. It is understandable that Hank has become somewhat cynical about investigative reporting. "With a few exceptions, most newspapers consider investigative reporters to be expendable," he says. "Newspapers like to use them on occasion for show but quickly silence them when they start to rock the boat. Organized crime would not be the problem it is today if more newspapers had lived up to their obligations to expose it."

An investigative reporter soon discovers that his unpopularity is not limited to the underworld. The other reporters in the city room may wonder why he writes a story only every six weeks or so while they have to grind one out every day, and why his stories get four columns of space in the paper while theirs with luck will get half a column.

Even the small rewards that sometimes come the way of an investigative reporter can prove elusive. For example, Jim Savage, a crack investigative reporter in Miami, not long ago was contacted by a Miami Beach civic group that planned to present him with its annual award for his contributions in fighting crime and corruption. Two days afterward Jim received a telephone call from a somewhat embarrassed group member who said that the group had changed its mind about the award. It seems that one of the men Jim had written about had promised the town a school bus, and when he heard that the group planned to honor Jim he issued an ultimatum: no award or no school bus.

Considering that an investigative reporter is treated like a pariah by so many of those around him, it is little wonder that most of the investigative reporters in the country form a close-knit fraternity. No matter how far apart they are geographically, they tend to keep in touch and will often help each other. For instance, when I went to St. Louis in 1968 to do a story on a powerful and corrupt union leader, the first person I contacted was Denny Walsh, then an investigative reporter for the St. Louis *Globe Democrat* (and now with *Life*) , who had been doing articles about the man's union for some time. Far from resenting my taking up a story that had been his alone, he was delighted to see the man exposed as widely as possible and gave me considerable help in researching my article.

Investigative reporters seem to be born, not made. The decision to go into this branch of journalism is not so much a conscious one as a combination of personality traits. This specialist must have an insatiable passion for digging out all the facts, no matter how dry and insignificant they might seem at first. This is in contrast to the reporter's usual motto: "Get what you can, then go with what you got." When a tantalizing story has come to an apparent dead end, the investigative reporter must be imaginative enough to believe that he will find a way to revive it. Finally, an investigative reporter must be lucky. It is a matter of being in the right place at the right time and then recognizing a potential story when it presents itself.

My very first investigative story, although I didn't consider it that at the time, in a small way illustrates all these elements. I was a sophomore at Boston University and had been reading a new biography of Eugene O'Neill by Arthur and Barbara Gelb. In the climactic scene, O'Neill is dying and directs his wife to burn the manuscripts of his unfinished plays in the fireplace of their Boston hotel room. I knew that the hotel had become a student dormitory, so I obtained permission from the student who lived there to look at the historic room. To my surprise, there was no evidence of a fireplace in the room. Out of curiosity I looked up blueprints of the building dating from its construction. Sure enough, there was no fireplace. This discrepancy seemed to me curious enough to warrant a small article in the

Boston University paper, of which I was then editor. The Gelbs heard of the piece, contacted me, and eventually took up the matter of the missing fireplace with O'Neill's widow. She admitted that, on second thought, perhaps she had burned the manuscripts in the basement.

The Gelbs corrected the book in its second edition, and although I soon forgot the incident, I had been bitten by the investigative bug. Ten years later, to the surprise of both of us, I found myself being hired at *The New York Times* by the same Arthur Gelb who had written the O'Neill biography and who had become the *Times*'s metropolitan editor.

Clearly, a man who makes investigative reporting his life must be strongly motivated by challenges and easily disturbed by unanswered questions. But there is one other quality that he must have in large measure, and it is more important than all the rest. It's what Bill Lambert calls "a low threshold of indignation."

Investigative reporters are no better and no worse than other men, but they must be more easily outraged by corruption, fraud, dishonesty, and the misuse of power than average citizens, because trying to expose these evils in some way is often their only reward.

1

YES, MR. RUDDY,
THERE IS
A MAFIA

ON MARCH 19, 1971, Albert S. Ruddy, producer of the film based on Mario Puzo's novel about the Mafia, *The Godfather,* announced that the words "Mafia" and "Cosa Nostra" would not be mentioned in the movie. "I'm Jewish so I know what prejudice and bigotry are," Mr. Ruddy told the members of the Italian-American Civil Rights League, whose leaders had persuaded him to censor the offending words.

Mr. Ruddy's announcement was applauded by the league as a great victory, but not all Italian-Americans saw it that way, including John Marchi, New York State senator. The censorship of the film script was "a monstrous insult to millions upon millions of loyal Americans of Italian extraction," Senator Marchi wrote Mr. Ruddy. "Apparently you are a ready market for the league's preposterous theory that we can exorcise devils by reading them out of the English language," he said. "Yes, Mr. Ruddy, there just might be a Mafia, and if you have been reached, I have only the feeling that the Italian-Americans as well as the larger community have been had."

As *The New York Times* pointed out in an editorial supporting Senator Marchi, the vast majority of Italian-Americans have no need to pretend that the Mafia does not exist in order to maintain their self-respect and a high standing in their communities. It is an insult to imply that their reputation as an ethnic group is so fragile that the mere mention of the words "Mafia" or "Costra Nostra" threatens it.

Others contend, however, that the words "Mafia" and "Cosa Nostra" should be eliminated from the language not because they constitute a slur but because they perpetuate a myth. This group includes not only men of questionable motives, such as members of organized crime. The Italian-American Civil Rights League, founded by Joseph Colombo, Sr., has received widespread support from thousands of individuals who have no underworld connections. Many of them honestly believe that the Mafia is a fiction created by the media and law enforcement agencies. Those who take this stand frequently raise the following three questions:

—If there is a Mafia, why hasn't the Federal Bureau of Investigation succeeded in infiltrating it as it has the Communist party, the Ku Klux Klan, and other groups under investigation?

—If there is a Mafia, why haven't any supposed members been caught using the word "Mafia" in conversations taped by police or federal agents?

—If there is a Mafia, why is Joseph Valachi, who gained much from the federal government, the only man to come forward and say he was a member of it?

People without a wide background of knowledge about organized crime will find these questions difficult to answer; but as arguments for the nonexistence of the Mafia they are fraudulent, because all three are based on misinformation.

The FBI, the Bureau of Narcotics and Dangerous Drugs, and other law enforcement agencies have successfully infiltrated the Mafia many times. For example, the kickback conspiracy involving New York City water commissioner James Marcus and a Mafioso named Antonio "Tony Ducks" Corallo was exposed in 1968 by Herbert Itkin, who developed close ties to Corallo and then informed the FBI. John Ormento and Carmine Galente, probably the Mafia's most successful heroin importers in the 1950's, are now serving long prison terms because they trusted a man named Edward L. Smith, who was a government informant.

It is true that the FBI has never sent an agent to join the Mafia and then talk publicly about what he found. In fact, as a matter of policy federal law enforcement agencies never permit their agents to become members of any organization in which they would be called upon to commit a serious crime, whether the organization is the Communist party, the Ku Klux Klan, the Black Panthers, or the Mafia.

The law enforcement agencies will, however, use members of such groups who offer to talk out of civic-mindedness, spite, revenge, or the desire to win a light sentence after having been arrested. The Bureau of Narcotics and Dangerous Drugs will even occasionally make an especially useful informant in a gang a "special employee" in order to pay him a regular salary for as long as they use him. The FBI, however, will not even do that, for it does not want a member of the underworld to become too familiar with its agents and operating procedures. But the FBI does pay informants, including past and present Mafiosi (who, understandably, do not "sing" as publicly as Joseph Valachi did).

No one has ever caught a Mafioso using the word "Mafia" even in monitored conversations with his fellow members simply because it is an old term long abandoned within the organization.

It has been replaced by numerous euphemisms, which often vary from city to city. In New York and other cities on the East Coast, as Valachi pointed out, the Mafia has been called Cosa Nostra ("Our Thing"). In Chicago it is often called The Outfit, in Buffalo The Arm, and in some parts of New England The Office. All these terms have come up in monitored conversations. But the public cannot be expected to keep up with these regional variations, and so it continues to use the time-honored term "Mafia."

As for Valachi's reward, the only payment he received from the government for singing in public was private prison accommodations and rigid security to protect him from his fellow inmates, permitting him to die in prison of natural causes. Furthermore, he is by no means the only Mafia member to talk in public about the organization.

During the 1918 murder trial of a New York Mafioso named Pelligrino Morano, the district attorney produced a witness named Tony Nataro, who talked at length about the Mafia, particularly about his own initiation into the organization:

> . . . a man named Tony the Shoemaker gave me a penknife . . . [and] extended his arm in this fashion [witness illustrates]. He said to me, "Strike here." I did with the penknife and just a little blood came out. Pelligrino bent over the Shoemaker's arm and sucked

the blood and a little blood came out. He said to me, "You have gained."

When Valachi was initiated in 1930, it was his own blood that was shed, but otherwise the ceremony was much the same:

> So Joe Bananas [Valachi's sponsor] . . . comes to me and says, "Give me that finger you shoot with." I hand him the finger, and he pricks the end of it with a pin and squeezes until the blood comes out. When that happens Mr. Maranzano [a Mafia boss] says, "This blood means that we are now one family." In other words, we are all tied up.

A third man to describe his experiences in the Mafia was Nicola Gentile, who did it neither in a courtroom like Nataro nor before a congressional committee like Valachi. There can be no question of pressure having been put upon him because his description is contained in the memoirs he wrote after retiring.

Gentile was born in Sicily in 1884 and came to the United States nineteen years later. He joined the Mafia and at various times served as a leader of families in Pittsburgh, Cleveland, and Kansas City. By the mid-1930's his fortunes had declined catastrophically, however, and he fled to Sicily to avoid trial on a narcotics charge.

He continued his involvement with the Mafia in Sicily, becoming an important figure in the black market there after World War II. He retired early in the 1950's and began writing about his experiences with the Mafia both in Sicily and in the United States. The memoirs, written in Italian, were never published, but parts of them were quoted in the Italian press along with interviews with Gentile, who made no secret of his Mafia membership.

Gentile left the United States in 1937 and had never heard of Valachi when he began setting down his memoirs. Where their accounts overlapped, Valachi's strongly supported Gentile's. Yet Valachi provided much more detail, and of course covered events that took place long after Gentile left the country, so Valachi could not have based his story on the older man's memoirs.

In addition to Valachi, Nataro, and Gentile, other Mafia members have broken the sacred law of silence and talked about the organization to which they belong. Their statements have not been made public by law enforcement officials because the men are considered too valuable for their lives to be endangered by public exposure. But lawmen have complete records of their disclosures as well as tapes of hundreds of hours of telephone conversation between Mafiosi.

When the public and private statements of members are pieced together it becomes compellingly clear that a secret organization, by whatever name it is called, took root in Italian soil many centuries ago, was eventually transplanted to American soil, and still thrives today as a key element in organized crime.

The Mafia had its beginnings in Palermo, Sicily, in 1282, when the natives rose against their French rulers in the rebellion known as the Sicilian Vespers and succeeded in freeing their country of foreign domination for a hundred years. The motto in that uprising was "Morte alla Francia Italia anela!" ("Death to the French is Italy's cry!") After the rebellion a secret organization was formed to protect poor Sicilians; it took its name from the first letters in the motto of the insurrection: MAFIA.

Sometime during the nineteenth century the character of the Mafia changed completely and its goals were reversed. Its members were then hired by rich landowners to keep the peasants in line. The Mafia men finally began to extort money and goods from the peasants directly. "All organizations are born with principles and humanitarian goals, but in their midst opportunities are never missing and men will always try to use them to make a profit," Nicola Gentile wrote later in discussing the history of the Mafia. In that way, he said, the Mafia became an organization "that finds its reason for existence in force and terror."

Mafiosi came to the United States with the first

34

wave of immigration at the end of the last century. The first recorded Mafia killing in the United States occurred on January 24, 1889, when a man named Vincenzo Ottumvo was murdered in New Orleans during a card game. A gang war followed that ultimately led to two grand jury investigations. The report of one jury concluded:

> The range of our researches has developed the existence of the secret organization styled "Mafia." The evidence comes from several sources fully competent in themselves to attest its truth, while the fact is supported by the long record of bloodcurdling crimes, it being almost impossible to discover the perpetrators or to secure witnesses.

By 1910 there were Mafia gangs in many major United States cities. Gentile offers the best picture of the organization in this early period. He relates that it preyed almost exclusively on newly arrived Italian immigrants and that its members were "ignorant and practically all illiterate." Mafia groups in those days were "very democratic," Gentile wrote. Groups of ten members chose leaders (*capos*), who in turn elected the head of the family (*capo famiglia*). The heads of families and their lieutenants elected the head of all the Mafia, who was known as the boss of bosses (*capo dei capi*), or king.

By the time Valachi testified, the organization of Mafia families had evolved somewhat. He said that each family included an underboss, who served as executive to the *capo*. Each lieutenant commanded a *regime,* or "crew," composed of "soldiers," whose status varied depending on experience, ability, and associations. He added that every member accepted in the Mafia had to be of Italian origin, although each family has many associates from every ethnic group who are "outsiders."

Both Valachi and Gentile said that Mafia leaders often waged bloody battles against one another, and that one of those wars had ultimately produced profound changes in the organization. That fight began in New York in 1930 and involved gangs led by Giuseppe Masseria and Salvatore Maranzano—two powerful Mafiosi who were Italian-born, ambitious, and eager to be boss of bosses.

Mafia leaders from other cities ultimately united behind a decision to end the war by having Masseria killed. Gentile's account of the killing parallels Valachi's: Masseria was lured to a restaurant by one of his most trusted aides, Salvatore Luciana, known as Lucky Luciano. After the meal, Luciano excused himself to go to the men's room. In his absence, four men walked into the restaurant and shot Masseria to death.

After the murder, Gentile wrote, Luciano and

the younger Mafia leaders wanted to replace the boss of bosses with a commission of several leaders. But Maranzano refused and found enough support among the older leaders, the Mustache Petes as they were called, to be named boss. Maranzano then plotted to have Luciano and his supporters eliminated, according to Gentile, but Luciano beat him to it. Maranzano was killed in his office on the afternoon of September 10, 1931. Gentile wrote that the killers were "six Jewish youths, assisted and accompanied by an Italian." Valachi said that they were "Meyer Lansky's boys," with an Italian sent along to identify Maranzano. Non-Italians had been used, he said, to divert attention from Luciano. (Lansky, whose career is detailed in Chapter 3, was a close friend of Luciano's and eventually rose to become one of the brains behind the financial affairs of organized crime.)

After the death of Maranzano, according to both Gentile and Valachi, younger Mafia leaders across the country eliminated many Mustache Petes in a single night of executions that came to be called the Night of the Sicilian Vespers. Neither Gentile nor Valachi said how many old Mafiosi were killed, but United States Attorney General Ramsey Clark in his book *Crime in America* put the figure at forty.

With Maranzano gone, control of the Mafia was unofficially in the hands of Lucky Luciano, the shrewd, cold-eyed, but soft-spoken racketeer who had earned his nickname as a young man by surviving hours of torture when he was kidnapped by rival hoodlums. He had refused to talk in spite of being tortured with razors and lighted cigarettes. His tormentors had left him to die, but he survived, and eventually became one of the most powerful bosses the Mafia has ever had.

Luciano purged Maranzano's followers and then set about improving the structure of the Mafia and expanding his own influence. He added the *consigliere* (counselor) to the Mafia family to mediate grievances and cut down on internal squabbling. He also helped set up a national *commissione* of Mafia bosses to arbitrate disputes between families, to confirm the appointment of new family bosses, and most important of all, to keep the various Mafia groups operating smoothly and successfully.

While Luciano thus provided for collective leadership, he nevertheless was "first among equals" and the most powerful man in the Mafia. Ensconced in a sumptuous suite in the Hotel Waldorf Astoria, he received a cut from the profits of every important Mafia racket in New York City.

Luciano was convicted by special prosecutor Thomas Dewey of multiple counts of compulsory prostitution and was sent to prison in 1936 (he was released and deported to Italy a decade later).

He was succeeded by his underboss Vito Genovese, but Genovese fled to Italy in 1937 to escape the heat that Dewey's investigation was still generating and was trapped there by the outbreak of World War II.

After the departure of Luciano and Genovese, Frank Costello came to dominate the Mafia. A dapper man who treated himself to a professional manicure and shave every day and dressed like an aristocrat, Costello proved to be as imaginative as he was sophisticated. He expanded the Mafia's involvement in legitimate business and secured for it valuable political connections. He doted on being seen with important politicians, and he became such a power in Tammany Hall, the New York Democratic organization, that a Tammany leader once remarked, "If Costello wanted me, he would send for me."

Costello, however, did not have the grim strength of Luciano; when Genovese returned to New York after the war, Costello allowed himself to be slowly squeezed out of power. An attempt on his life in 1957 persuaded him to retire to the sidelines and leave the field to Genovese, a Neapolitan by birth, who, although his education had ceased in the fifth grade, was noted for the Byzantine complexity of his mind as well as for his brutality.

Soon after taking power in New York, Genovese called a conclave of Mafia leaders from all over the

United States in order to justify his displacement of Costello and to expand his prestige outside New York City. He also wanted the bosses to work out a policy about the Mafia's involvement in narcotics, because an increasing number of members were drawing long prison terms for narcotics violations.

The meeting was held at the home of Joseph Barbara in Apalachin, New York, on November 14, 1957, but it had barely gotten under way when state police began to close in on the house. The Mafiosi quickly scattered into the nearby woods and a number of them escaped, but the police picked up sixty of the others.

Since 1957 police have been aware of a number of other, smaller Mafia conclaves, usually dubbed "Little Apalachins." Lawmen have interrupted one such meeting in a Forest Hills, New York, restaurant in 1966, and another in Palm Springs, California, in 1965, but they have learned about others only after the fact. Sadder but wiser Mafia bosses have not repeated their mistake of meeting in a private home, and they have kept their conclaves regional rather than national in scope. Nevertheless, Apalachin and succeeding meetings indicate that the Mafia families across the country are indeed linked to each other, even though they operate independently in their own areas.

The Mafia leaders picked up at Apalachin could

not be convicted on any charges, but six months later Genovese was arrested and accused of conspiracy to violate federal narcotics laws. He was convicted in 1959 and sentenced to fifteen years in prison. While at the Atlanta Penitentiary in 1962 he came to the conclusion that Joseph Valachi, a soldier in his Mafia family and a fellow inmate, was an informer.

On a June day in 1962, Genovese gave Valachi the "kiss of death," starting a series of events that would make the heavyset Valachi, with his steel-gray crew cut, his square face and bulbous nose, a familiar sight on the television screens of America as he testified in his raspy, chain-smoker's voice about the internal workings of the Mafia.

At the time that he received the kiss of death, Valachi had not told the authorities anything, but Genovese refused to believe his indignant denials. Frightened and desperate, Valachi used an iron pipe to beat to death a fellow inmate who he wrongly thought had been chosen to be his executioner. Valachi was sentenced to life imprisonment for the murder, and feeling betrayed by Genovese, he began to tell authorities about the Cosa Nostra. Valachi acted out of selfish motives —anger and a desire for revenge—and he was in no way a hero. But the vivid and detailed picture that he painted of the Mafia made Americans see how the organization's activities menace American society. Public concern in turn stimulated law enforcement agencies to step up their campaigns against organized crime and to coordinate their efforts in fighting it.

Thus the Mafia, and organized crime as a whole, is weaker today than it was in 1962 when Joseph Valachi began to tell his story. The Mafia is still a formidable and threatening force, but a number of the men Valachi identified as members are now in prison and many more are under indictment. Several others have died or have been killed. As a result, the leadership of the Mafia has changed considerably since Valachi testified. For example, of the men he identified as bosses of New York's five families, three have died—Thomas Luchese, Joseph Magliocco, and Vito Genovese—and a fourth, Joseph Bonanno, has been deposed. Only Carlo Gambino survives, as powerful as ever.

There are twenty-six Mafia families operating in twenty-one metropolitan areas in the United States (see chart following the last chapter). Of the estimated 5,000 full-fledged Mafia members, about 2,000 belong to the five families in the New York metropolitan area, the only area in the country with more than one family. No new members have been inducted since 1957, partly out of fear that increasingly effective federal law enforcement agencies will infiltrate enough informants into the families to destroy the Mafia. As a result, families have been recruiting a growing number of "associates"—men who work in Mafia rackets but are not members and are not privy to the secrets that go with membership.

Joseph Valachi died of a heart attack on April 3, 1971, at the age of sixty-seven, just as the validity of his information was increasingly being challenged. His critics charge that he had either made up everything or had been told a lot of half-truths, rumors, and lies by the FBI to repeat to the world as inside information. This criticism was part of the general campaign to raise doubts that the Mafia exists at all. Such an effort is based on wishful thinking rather than on reality. The evidence that the Mafia exists is as compelling as the fact that Italian-Americans have no need to pretend it does not. It is just as wrong, and as dangerous, to deny the Mafia's existence as it is to claim that all gangsters are Italian.

Joseph Valachi, himself the son of an Italian immigrant, was bewildered when he was told that his testimony had raised a clamor of protest from Italian-Americans who felt that he was smearing them and their ancestors. "I'm not talking about Italians," Valachi explained. "I'm talking about criminals."

2

NO, MR. PUZO, YOU DON'T HAVE TO BE ITALIAN TO BE IN ORGANIZED CRIME

BEFORE *The Godfather* made Mario Puzo a best-selling novelist, he often wrote magazine articles; one of his favorite subjects was organized crime. In an article published in *The New York Times Magazine* in 1967, Puzo wrote: "But do Italians and American-Italians control organized crime in America? The answer must be a reluctant but firm Yes. . . . Most of the operators in organized crime in this country will bleed Italian blood. That fact must be accepted. . . ."

The Mafia is certainly the most visible segment of organized crime—the most fascinating, the oldest, and the one most often written about. But to say that organized crime is almost exclusively Italian is simply wrong, although it is easy to see how Puzo could come to such a conclusion. He is of Italian extraction and has heard about the Mafia all his life. And he is from New York, where the Mafia is clearly the dominant force in organized crime.

To the west and south of such Mafia-dominated cities as New York, Buffalo, and Detroit, there are many metropolitan areas dominated by non-Italian gangs of racketeers, and in some cities the Mafia does not exist at all. Crime in the United States is by no means a monopoly of Italians, although it sometimes seems that way because of the Mafia's dramatic history, colorful trappings and ceremonies, tightly knit organization, and conspicuous leaders.

Ever since the first immigrants landed in this country and began pushing westward, every ethnic group has contributed representatives to the underworld. In every crowded city more or less loosely organized gangs of criminals vied with each other. They shanghaied sailors for clippers, forced girls into prostitution, robbed banks and trains, stole horses and rustled cattle. But what we now call organized crime—the national federation of criminal gangs that operate in America today—is believed to be less than fifty years old and to have its roots in Prohibition.

From January 16, 1920, when the Volstead Act went into effect, until the repeal of Prohibition in 1933, the efforts of criminals to circumvent the law passed through three distinct phases. The first involved stealing alcohol intended for legitimate purposes, such as the manufacture of cough syrups and hair tonics, and using it to make liquor. Many gangs in major industrial cities were involved in this racket, but they operated exclusively on a local level.

During the next phase the liquor known as rotgut was manufactured from corn sugar in thousands of small stills. The distribution of the rotgut was controlled by gangs operating in specific territories, although the boundaries of these territories were frequently disputed in gang wars.

Organized crime as we know it today came into being during the third phase of Prohibition—rum-running. During this period good whisky was smuggled into the country from Europe, Canada, and the Bahamas.

Organized crime owes a great deal to the Volstead Act. While that law was in force heads of local criminal gangs found themselves dealing with immense sums of money. This situation provided "on the job training" that turned some of them into executives as expert as the heads of major legitimate businesses. And the man on the street, who broke the law daily as a matter of course by drinking at his favorite speakeasy, began to develop a tolerance for lawbreakers. It was this casual familiarity that eventually surrounded gangsters with the aura of picaresque glamour that still exists in the public mind today.

Profits from rumrunning were immense because of the great demand for good whisky. But importing the whisky, transporting it to various cities, and then distributing it within those cities made it essential to have cooperation between gangs.

The potential of rumrunning was first glimpsed by a foresighted New York gangster named Irving Wexler, better known as Waxey Gordon. But he realized that to buy huge amounts of whisky abroad would require considerable cash, and to distribute it in New York would require political protection. So he went to the only man who could be counted on for both: Arnold Rothstein.

By the mid-1920's Rothstein was the most famous gambler in America. He was smooth, softspoken, and noted for a degree of nervous energy that rarely let him sleep. He would play dice all night and then put in a fifteen-hour day at his office juggling his many enterprises, which included enormous real estate holdings. He was trailed everywhere by one or two bodyguards, but he was distinguished by his fine manners and prided himself on the number of his friends who were listed in the *Social Register*.

Rothstein's legend reached its peak in 1919,

when he was suspected of fixing the World Series. During his career he faced many indictments, including concealment and perjury on his income tax returns and felonious assault when three policemen were shot at. But throughout a life of legal tangles, Rothstein was never convicted of doing anything dishonest. He insisted that his vast fortune—estimated between two and ten million—and his huge gambling winnings (he made $500,000 on the first Dempsey-Tunney fight) were exclusively the result of his superior mental ability. "The majority of the human race are dumbbells," he once said.

It is not surprising that Waxey Gordon chose Rothstein as the man with both the power and the vision to set up a vast rumrunning empire, and Rothstein did not let him down. He quickly built up an organization to buy liquor in England and sell it in New York. He was so successful that others followed his example.

As the competition grew, Rothstein stopped bringing in his own whisky and started hijacking his rivals' liquor shipments on their way to distribution points. For this purpose he used such gunmen as Legs Diamond (real name: John T. Noland) and Dutch Schultz (Arthur Flegenheimer). Rothstein ultimately gave up bootlegging and went back to his first love, gambling. On November 4, 1929, he was shot to death in his hotel suite. The crime has never been solved.

Rothstein's legacy to the underworld was a series of gang wars sparked by the hijackings he had started. As the rumrunners tried to wipe each other out, everyone's profits declined sharply. A few of the gang leaders began to realize that some form of cooperation had to be worked out. By this time gangland killings had become so common that pedestrians in large cities were not surprised to see men mowed down on street corners by bursts of machine-gun fire issuing from black limousines. In Chicago alone, during a four-year period in the twenties, there were two hundred unsolved underworld murders. Said Lucky Luciano after a visit to the city: "A real goddamn crazy place! Nobody's safe in the streets."

In New York Luciano and several other underworld leaders decided that there was much more to gain by cooperating with each other than by fighting continuously. Late in the 1920's they formed an alliance that has been dubbed the Eastern Syndicate. It included members from many ethnic groups: Anglo-Saxons such as Owney "The Killer" Madden, Irishmen such as William "Big Bill" Dwyer, Jews such as Meyer Lansky, and younger Mafiosi such as Luciano. Such cooperation did not come easily. The older Mustache Petes in the Mafia had traditionally been opposed to the idea of working with non-Italian gangs, even though some of these non-Italians had greater expertise in bootlegging than the Mafia.

Soon the new syndicate in New York began to establish ties with gangs in other Eastern cities. These included a group from Boston dominated by Charles "King" Solomon and a number of New Jersey gangsters known as the Reinfeld Syndicate. The Reinfeld Syndicate had achieved such success at importing whisky from Canada that it eventually became the principal supplier for "rum rows" (streets of illegal speakeasies) all along the northeast coast.

While gangs in the Northeast were forging links, regional syndicates in other parts of the country were also slowly learning the value of cooperation. In the Cleveland area a group called the Mayfield Road Mob joined other gangs to form a federation called the Cleveland Syndicate, which brought whisky from Canada to rum rows all along Lake Erie. The Cleveland Syndicate was dominated by four men—Samuel Tucker, Morris Dalitz, Morris Kleinman, and Louis Rothkopf—but key figures in the notorious mob included an Irishman, Tom McGinty, and three Italians, Frank Milano, Al Polizzi, and Joe Massei.

The effect of the syndicate on Cleveland during Prohibition was described twenty years later to the Kefauver Committee by Alvin Sutton, Director of Public Safety in Cleveland. "They had their suppliers of Canadian whisky and their salesmen and thugs to distribute the contraband and to reap the harvest of money . . ." Sutton testified.

"Ruthless beatings, unsolved murders and shakedowns and threats and bribery came to the community as a result of the gangsters' rise to power."

West of Cleveland, the Minneapolis Combination, another federation, brought Canadian whisky across Lake Superior and distributed it throughout Minnesota and Wisconsin. The leading gang in this syndicate was called the Kid Cann Mob after the nickname of its leader, Isadore Blumenfield.

Kid Cann earned a formidable underworld reputation during Prohibition and later. His gang was linked to two of Minnesota's most famous murders during the 1930's, but it was not convicted of either. In 1934 the editor of a newspaper called the *Saturday Press* announced over the radio that he intended to expose the close ties between Minnesota politicians and such underworld figures as Kid Cann. The following night, as he was leaving a fruit stand, the editor was shot down from an automobile. His face was torn off by the shells. The campaign was taken up by Walter Liggett, publisher of the *Midwest American*. In 1936, as Liggett stepped from his car with his wife and daughter, he was killed by machine-gun fire that came from an automobile moving in the opposite direction. His widow and another witness swore that they recognized the murderer as Kid Cann himself, but at his trial the Kid was acquitted. He said he had been in a barbershop seven-

teen blocks away and produced numerous wit-
nesses to support his story. At the trial J. M. Sim-
mons, a special investigator for the Minnesota
Law and Order League, described how well gangs
in Minneapolis cooperated with each other. Sim-
mons said that the city had been divided into
four districts, "each with its capital, its captain,
lieutenant and fixer." He said that hoodlums
from a number of gangs worked amicably within
the framework.

Even in Chicago, which was considered the personal fiefdom of Al Capone, bootlegging and other
rackets were pursued by a federation of gangs. A
degree of cooperation was painfully achieved
after the leaders of the various gangs, tiring of
the carnage that long had bloodied Chicago's
streets, held a conference in the Hotel Sherman
on October 21, 1926, and called an end to all out-
standing feuds.

The names of the participants at the conference
make it clear that Chicago's organized underworld was not run exclusively by Italians. Besides
Capone, the men sitting around the table included Bugs Moran, Maxie Eisen, Christian
Bertche, William Skidmore, Jack Zuta, and Frank
Foster. The peace conference held at the Hotel
Sherman did not instantly end all gang warfare in
Chicago—as the St. Valentine's Day Massacre
dramatically illustrated eighteen months later
when Capone gunmen killed seven members of

a rival group. But in spite of the massacre, the spirit of cooperation eventually cooled gang rivalries in Chicago and continues to this day.

During Prohibition, alliances between criminal groups also developed in several other cities including St. Louis, Missouri, where gangsters of Syrian extraction dominated, and Savannah, Georgia, where a coalition of gangs very effectively supplied whisky to cities all along the southern Atlantic coast.

Regional syndicates often joined in purchasing huge quantities of whisky in Canada and then dividing it after it was smuggled into the United States. So effective were these group efforts that the repeal of Prohibition in 1933 in no way weakened the bonds that linked the gangs. Many of the regional syndicates shifted their interests from bootlegging to gambling, loan-sharking, labor racketeering, and other illegal ventures. And many groups became active in the newly legal liquor industry.

Cross-country cooperation paid off for the underworld in many ways. The leaders of the syndicates cooperated in setting up wire services that instantly provided the results of races at tracks all over the country. There was such potential for the numbers rackets in many ghetto and immigrant neighborhoods that a number of different gangs could harmoniously divide up the action. And gangs joined in financing illegal gambling casinos in communities where law enforcement was lax.

For example, when Meyer Lansky and Frank Costello opened illegal casinos in upstate New York, New Orleans, and southern Florida, they cut in several of their colleagues from the Cleveland, Minneapolis, and Savannah syndicates. When the leaders of the Mayfield Road Mob in Cleveland moved over to Newport, Kentucky, and turned it into a wide-open gambling paradise, they invited gangsters from half a dozen cities into the action.

Through the years these top gangsters pooled their financial expertise to put their profits from the rackets to work in legitimate businesses. Some of the choicest land in Miami Beach and some of the tallest buildings in Manhattan came under their ownership either openly or through front men. The racketeers also bought into legitimate businesses, often bleeding them of valuable assets and letting them fall into ruin.

When the potential of Las Vegas became clear late in the 1940's, leaders of nearly all the Prohibition-era syndicates were quick to invest in the casinos there. Some of the same men—Meyer Lansky, Frank Costello, Sam Tucker—also put money into the casinos that flourished in Havana, Cuba, before Fidel Castro took control of the island. Although Mafia members were conspicuous in both Las Vegas and Havana, they were in the minority there compared to the underworld figures from other ethnic groups.

Even in New York, the Mafia's home ground, a number of non-Mafiosi have done quite well in the underworld. One of the biggest gambling figures in the city is Hugh Mulligan, and two of the most powerful numbers operators are brothers Sam and Moe Schlitten. Prominent labor racketeers in the city in recent years have included not only such Mafiosi as Anthony DiLorenzo and John Dioguardi, but also such non-Italians as Jack McCarthy and David Wenger.

Clearly, the underworld in the United States is as much a melting pot as any other aspect of our culture, and the opportunities for vice have attracted just as many ethnic groups as the opportunities for legitimate achievement. Since the days of Jesse James and Billy the Kid, Americans have loved flamboyant criminals. Perhaps that is why it is so difficult to see beyond the Mafia, with its old traditions and its "Italians only" membership. But anyone who takes a searching look at the web of crime that stretches over the United States will have to take issue with Mario Puzo. Many of the operators in organized crime in this country will not bleed Italian blood. And if every member of the Mafia disappeared tomorrow, organized crime would still be an immense, if largely invisible, parasite sucking the lifeblood of American society.

3

MEYER LANSKY—
UNDERWORLD
GENIUS

WHEN MAIER SUCHOWJANSKY arrived on Ellis Island from Grodno, Russia, in 1911, his mother, in all the confusion, could not remember the day or even the month in which he had been born nine years earlier. So the immigration officials gave him July 4 as a birth date, hoping, perhaps, to instill in the boy a sense of patriotism and high aspirations.

In many ways Maier Suchowjansky, who Americanized his name to "Meyer Lansky," lived up to those hopes. He became so patriotic that he moved heaven and earth to get his oldest son into West Point. He is as ardent a supporter of United

States involvement in Vietnam as any man in America. As for material success, he set his aspirations high and has achieved the directorship of a network of enterprises as big as General Motors. His personal fortune is estimated to be somewhere between $100 million and $300 million.

The thing that sets Meyer Lansky apart from most men who have achieved the American Dream is his line of business. He chose to pursue his ambitions not in steel or oil, not in automobiles or banking, but in crime. In that field he is as much of a visionary and innovator as Andrew Carnegie, Henry Ford, and John D. Rockefeller were in theirs. Lansky is the main architect of the giant conglomerate that is organized crime in the United States. Forty years ago he helped pull together a group of rival gangs, including the Mafia, into a national network and then proceeded to shape it into a silent, streamlined colossus that is now, in his own words, "bigger than U.S. Steel."

As a director of the organized crime syndicate, of which the Mafia is the biggest branch, Lansky is so powerful that he controls legitimate corporations, runs a gambling network that stretches from Las Vegas to the Middle East, and "buys" whole governments with bribes. Even the United States Navy once had to plead for his help.

He has convinced the syndicate that it should de-emphasize such high-risk enterprises as narcotics, prostitution, and murder-by-contract and enter new fields such as banking, investments, manufacturing, and real estate by using thousands of fronts, some so sophisticated they may never be penetrated. In addition, he has developed new ways to promote the underworld's most lucrative traditional source of income— gambling—in the Caribbean, England, Europe, and the Middle East.

Lansky the man is a fascinating series of contradictions. His personal style is radically different from that of the cigar-smoking professional mobster portrayed by Edward G. Robinson in *Little Caesar* or by Rod Steiger in *Al Capone*. At sixty-nine, Lansky is gray-haired, thin, even ascetic in appearance. In many ways he is indistinguishable from a successful Scarsdale investment broker on a two-week Miami Beach vacation. His suits are conservatively cut, and his home, until 1969, was a modest three-bedroom ranch-style house in Hallandale, Florida, a suburb of Miami. He drives rented Chevrolets, walks the family dog, and goes home every night to his wife. He brags about the grandchildren, takes his wife with him on annual vacations, and carefully shields her from contacts with his underworld friends. On the few occasions when he has been pushed into the public spotlight, Lansky has shown occasional flashes of dry humor and a quiet, relaxed demeanor.

Early in 1969 Lansky sold the house in Hallandale and moved to a beachfront apartment building with tight security at 5001 Collins Avenue in Miami Beach, a short walk from the Fontainebleau and Eden Roc hotels. He reportedly made the move because he feared that the suburban home exposed him to the danger of being kidnapped for ransom by the "young Turks" in the underworld, a fate that had befallen certain New York gang leaders late in 1968.

In the summer of 1970 Lansky moved to Israel and settled down in a suite in the Dan Hotel in Tel Aviv. At about the same time federal agents were investigating the skimming of millions of dollars worth of gambling profits from the Flamingo Hotel in Las Vegas from 1960 to 1967.

In March, 1971, Lansky was indicted by a federal grand jury in Miami of conspiring to engage in illegal gambling activity and to conceal proceeds from the Flamingo Hotel. Lansky, of course, declined to return to the United States to face the charges.

When he was still in the country and the law began to crowd him, Lansky resorted to a favorite ploy: he pretended to be deathly ill. Whenever the heat was on—an investigation made public, a grand jury inquiry, a new task force of federal crime fighters on his trail—the story circulated that Lansky was dying of cancer or some other terminal illness. A report in the files of the New York State police, dating from the 1920's, states that there is no need to worry about Meyer Lansky's criminal activities because he will not live for more than a year. The police report, to say the least, was greatly exaggerated. Lansky today is in the pink of health and looks ten years younger than his age. "He'll probably live to be one hundred," says an old friend and former racketeer.

Acting like any good businessman with a social conscience, Lansky makes occasional contributions to reputable charities. But the contributions are always small—between $2,500 and $5,000—in keeping with Lansky's image. Lansky has made at least two small contributions to Brandeis University at the behest of his friend Joseph Linsey, a Boston businessman with underworld links who is a large contributor to the university. Lansky treasures a 1962 letter from Abram Sachar, former president of Brandeis, thanking him for a contribution arranged by Linsey.

Even Lansky's tax returns, it is said, portray a retired investor living in moderate comfort off the returns from a few prudent holdings. Lansky can justify every penny of every expenditure; indeed he often does not even take the deductions to which he is entitled.

His holdings include $90,000 worth of oil and gas leases, which he bought in 1960 from Sam Garfield, a Michigan businessman who, over the years, has been associated in a number of deals with Lansky. To justify the sudden possession of such a large amount of cash, Lansky made it known first that he had received a loan from a friend for $90,000, and then he started making payments to Garfield for the leases. He is still drawing dividends from this investment, which is quite legal and helps him justify some of his modest expenditures.

Another ploy he used to justify an increase in his income came to light in November, 1969. The Toronto *Telegram* told the story of a bemused Toronto stockbroker who, not knowing who Lansky was, arranged to purchase $250 worth of mining claims in Canada for him. Four months later, Lansky had the broker handle the sale of the same mining claims to two New York brothers for $40,000. Lansky subsequently claimed the $38,750 "profit" on the deal as a capital gain and paid tax on it, much to the dismay of the Internal Revenue Service. The IRS believes that Lansky himself gave the brothers the $40,000 to buy the claims and thereby legitimatize, or "dry-clean," nearly $40,000 of mob profits. Because the deal had taken place in Canada, the IRS had no legal recourse.

In spite of being rich and powerful, Lansky maintains his modest life style down to the last detail, and with good reason. He has only to remember the fate of his more flamboyant colleagues to realize what happens to gangsters who flaunt their wealth. He started out in the rackets with such men as Joe Adonis, Frank Costello, Vito Genovese, Louis Lepke, Lucky Luciano, Dutch Schultz, and Bugsy Siegel. All loved to let their money show, and all wound up executed, assassinated, deported, imprisoned, or deposed.

So Lansky hides his wealth and courts anonymity with a passion worthy of Howard Hughes. He does not even bother to answer requests for interviews, and when he takes a walk, he never ventures more than a two-minute trot from his doorway. When he was still living in Miami Beach, I drove by his apartment building while he was taking a stroll, but as soon as he saw my car slow to a stop, he ran back into the building. He seldom went out then, and when he did it was only to restaurants and clubs operated by old friends in the rackets. Word went out early that "Joe Meyer" (Lansky's favorite code name) would be visiting that evening. A quiet table in a dark corner would then be reserved for him.

He likes plain food and one, at most two, bourbons before dinner. He has never been a heavy drinker or a ladies' man. He smokes cigars after meals and cigarettes in between. He is greatly concerned about the health dangers associated with cigarettes, but he has not managed to quit. He does not like the taste of filtered cigarettes, so he uses a three-inch cigarette holder, which he believes helps keep out tar and nicotine.

Lansky's main pleasures are simple. He likes to

travel, to go for walks, and to lie in the sun. Often he can be seen stretched out on a reclining chair by the swimming pool of his hotel, soaking up the sun. He is only 5 feet 4 inches tall, and in swimming trunks he loses his otherwise rather imposing presence. He likes to walk so much that he sometimes interrupts his business conferences to go for a stroll on the beach.

Like many other self-made millionaires, Lansky is distinctly right-wing politically. On Vietnam, for example, "he thinks we should go in there and blow Hanoi to pieces," according to an acquaintance. "He's really disgusted with all these demonstrations against the war."

Lansky's fervent conservatism and anti-Communism may have something to do with the end that Fidel Castro put to his flourishing gambling setup in Cuba in 1959. But at least one federal agent believes that a right-wing outlook is concomitant with underworld success. "A lot of your mob chiefs are fierce conservatives," he says. "They're guys who came to this country with nothing and who did very well here, who found this a land of plenty. So, in the right-wing sense of the word, they're quite the ardent patriots."

Lansky is so patriotic, in fact, that in 1949 he used all the political influence at his command to win an appointment to West Point for his oldest son, Paul. The appointment was made by the late New York State Supreme Court Justice

Arthur G. Klein, who was then a congressman. Paul Lansky did fairly well at the academy and rose to the rank of captain in the Air Force before resigning in 1963 to begin an engineering career on the West Coast. He now lives in Tacoma, Washington, with his wife and children and is a respected member of his community. To keep Paul's life from being affected by the Lansky name, Meyer has spread the rumor that his son broke with him several years ago and that they have not spoken to each other in a long time. This is not true, however. Lansky talks frequently with Paul on the telephone, and speaks proudly to his friends of the kind of life Paul has made for himself.

Lansky has two other children, a son named Bernard and a daughter, Sandra. Bernard, who is known as Buddy, lives in a comfortable house near his father's old home in Hallandale, Florida, and is often seen in supervisory positions in hotels and motels in which Meyer is said to have an interest. Lansky is very close to Bernard, who has been physically handicapped since childhood, and spends a lot of time with him.

Lansky's daughter, Sandra, has been married twice and had a reputation as a swinger when she was young. During that period she got into scrapes that gave her father more than a few sleepless nights. One of the scrapes would have gotten Lansky into trouble with his Mafia colleagues if he had not been so highly thought of in the underworld.

Most Italians in the underworld share the opinion of Angelo "Gyp" De Carlo, who, in a phone conversation taped by the FBI in New Jersey, referred to Lansky as the most respected non-Italian in the underworld. "There's only two Jews recognized in the whole country today," he said. "That's Meyer and . . . Moe Dalitz, but he [Dalitz] ain't got much recognition." (Dalitz is one of the founders of the uniquely successful "Cleveland Syndicate" and one of the men responsible for supervising the underworld's investments in Las Vegas.)

Lansky is easily the most heeded leader in the underworld, and for several good reasons. First, he has survived longer than anyone else in the underworld. In his fifty years in crime he has spent only three months in jail. Second, anyone who has associated himself with Lansky has made big money. Third, and most important, Lansky has the best brain in the underworld.

While he was still living in the United States, Lansky made annual trips to Europe with his wife and managed to combine business with pleasure. In his hotel rooms, where he spent most of his time, the syndicate's overseas representatives came to report to the chairman. Mrs. Lansky was never introduced to any of these men, and the meetings were never held in her presence.

These and other signs indicate that Lansky keeps his wife, an attractive sometime blonde twenty years his junior, at least partially in the dark about his real wealth and position. On the rare occasions when they go out together, he is careful to tip much less than when he is with friends or dining alone. When a reporter knocked at the Lansky home a few years ago, Mrs. Lansky informed him through the screen door that her husband was "misunderstood by the press and the FBI."

It was Lansky who developed the worldwide network of couriers, middlemen, bankers, and front men that allows the underworld to take profits from illegal enterprises, send them halfway around the world, and then have the money come back laundered clean to be invested in legitimate businesses.

The way this works is beautifully simple. Lansky's couriers take the Mafia's "black money"—profits from illegal activities—to secret bank accounts in Switzerland, where the money is "washed clean in the snow of the Alps," as the joke goes. Middlemen in Europe send the money from the Swiss accounts back to the United States as mortgages and loans, and on other legal pretexts. This "clean money" is then used for legitimate investments. There is no way to find out the ultimate source of the money because it can be traced back only to the Swiss banks, which will not divulge the names of depositors.

Occasionally, however, one can glimpse the faces of the men behind the underworld's money-laundering operations, and law enforcement officials are not surprised to find that many of those faces are easily recognizable as close friends and associates of Meyer Lansky.

Early in 1967, for example, a group of gangsters tried to defraud the Chase Manhattan Bank of almost $2 million, using the Exchange Bank of Geneva, Switzerland, as a cover. The scheme was uncovered before the money was transferred to the Geneva bank. An investigation ultimately resulted in an indictment of the Exchange Bank as a co-conspirator in the caper. It was revealed that the Swiss bank had served as a "laundry shop" for Mafia money for years. It was also discovered that the bank was owned by a group of Americans. The two principal owners were businessmen with clean records. But other owners included Edward Levinson, the Las Vegas casino operator who fronts for the Lansky syndicate, and Benjamin Siegelbaum, another Lansky associate.

In Europe Lansky's chief watchdog and head of operations is John Pullman, a former bootlegger who started out in the rackets with Lansky in the 1920's. Pullman was born in Rumania, naturalized an American citizen, and then denaturalized in

1954. He became a Canadian citizen, and finally moved to Switzerland as Lansky's chief overseas representative. He lives in Lausanne, but is always shuttling to Geneva, Rome, Paris, London, and Toronto for meetings with Lansky's representatives.

Meyer Lansky got an early start in crime. He was first picked up by the police when he was sixteen. By the time he was twenty-seven he had been arrested five times on charges ranging from disorderly conduct to suspicion of homicide. But not once were the police able to make the charges stick. An incident in 1926 explains why. A man named John Barrett was found near death from bullet wounds in a New York alley and rushed to a hospital. When he recovered consciousness, he told the police he had been shot and then pushed from a car by Lansky because of an argument over the loot from a warehouse robbery. Barrett agreed to testify against Lansky and was placed under heavy guard. When he discovered that his hospital food had been laced with arsenic, however, he decided that he could not rely on police protection and he bought his life by refusing to sign a complaint against his assailant.

By this time Lansky had become a close friend and partner of Benjamin "Bugsy" Siegel's. The short and hawk-faced Lansky so admired the tall, boyishly handsome Siegel that he borrowed his idol's nickname, and for a while called himself

Bugs Meyer. They first hired themselves out as gunmen to Legs Diamond and then started their own gang. The Bugs and Meyer Mob, as it was called, did a thriving business protecting liquor shipments from hijackers for the various gangs then operating in New York and New Jersey.

When various East Coast gangs formed an alliance to coordinate rumrunning on the Eastern seaboard, Siegel and Lansky were made members of the governing board. Lansky was appointed controller of the merged group, which came to be known as the Eastern Syndicate.

Early in the 1930's, as was pointed out in Chapter 2, the Eastern Syndicate began to link up with the Cleveland and Reinfeld syndicates—groups that specialized in smuggling bootleg booze from Canada—and other regional mobs to form a national syndicate. The tie-in with the Cleveland Syndicate provided important lessons in Lansky's education as a gangster. The four leaders of this group—Moe Dalitz, Morris Kleinman, Sam Tucker, and the late Louis Rothkopf—were more subtle, and often more effective, than crime leaders in the East. They relied more on the bribe than the bullet, led inconspicuous personal lives, and hid behind numerous and effective fronts. Lansky was to study their methods, refine them, and use them to lead organized crime in the United States into a new era.

But all that took time. In the 1930's Lansky and

his underworld associates were still toiling in the usual vineyards—narcotics, prostitution, hijacking, extortion, gambling. For a time Lansky, Bugsy Siegel, Louis Lepke, and Lucky Luciano ran a factory in the Bronx section of New York to extract morphine from an opium base for the illicit drug market. Each man had other things going and none took it too hard when this project failed to fulfill its early promise. Lepke, for one, teamed up with Gurrah Shapiro to recruit a group of vicious contract killers such as Albert Anastasia and Abe Reles into the infamous Murder Inc. That organization served as the enforcement arm of the new Eastern Syndicate, which had succeeded the Bugs and Meyer Mob. But Lepke, an inventive man, broadened the base of Murder Inc. and offered murder as a marketable service to all comers.

Murder Inc. ended the lives of an estimated eight hundred persons before prosecutors Burton Turkus and the late Thomas E. Dewey moved forcefully against the New York mobs some thirty-five years ago. Their racket-busting almost shattered the Eastern Syndicate altogether, and several of its leaders stayed as far as possible from New York while the investigations were in progress.

Bugsy Siegel went to Hollywood, California, where he socialized with the movie stars he had always envied. (He shook down a number of them, but was so popular anyhow that Jean Har-

low became godmother to two of his children.)
Lansky went to Hollywood, Florida, although he
returned often to New York, where he kept an
apartment until 1953.

Lucky Luciano, the top man at the time, refused
to leave the center of his operations at all. He was
ultimately convicted by Dewey on so many counts
of white slavery that he was sentenced to fifty
years in prison.

Dewey thus eliminated some of the syndicate's
most powerful members, but indirectly he did the
organization a favor. Under the pressure of his investigation many of the remaining leaders, who
had become rather parochial, left New York,
spread their operations, and made the syndicate
truly national.

Lansky, for one, built a whole new empire in
southern Florida and the Caribbean by imitating
the Cleveland group, particularly in the use of
bribes to secure the cooperation of police officials
and politicians.

The efficiency of the bribes was dramatized in
the Kefauver Committee hearings in 1953. Walter Clark, sheriff of Broward County, Florida,
from 1933 to 1952, admitted, for example, that he
not only provided "special policing" for Lansky's
illegal gambling establishments but also deputized
the men who drove armored cars carrying cash
from casinos to the bank.

In 1937 Lansky explored the possibility of expanding his operations to Cuba. He found a willing listener in Fulgencio Batista, the former army sergeant then in power, and the two made plans for turning Havana into a playground for the rich. World War II, however, put an end to this initial effort. "There weren't any boats on the seas," Lansky later told the Kefauver Committee. "You can't live from the Cuban people themselves."

During the war Lansky played a key role in one of the strangest deals in which the United States government has ever been involved. The full story has never been told; but as it was outlined during the Kefauver hearings, naval intelligence decided that it needed the help of the Mafia to protect East Coast shipping from sabotage. Lucky Luciano was the only man who could arouse the Mafia to such service, but he was still in prison—and not likely to be feeling patriotic.

The Navy turned to Luciano's attorney, Moses Polakoff, who promised to talk to his client. But he said that he had to take along someone whom Luciano would trust—Meyer Lansky. For several months Polakoff and Lansky visited Luciano regularly and ultimately, as Polakoff recalled in 1970, Luciano "agreed to be of whatever service he could. He passed the word along." (Luciano owed Lansky a big favor. As was outlined in Chapter 1, when Luciano was trying to rise to the top of the Mafia, Lansky made room for him by having some of his men kill the then head of the group, Salvatore Maranzano.)

How much Luciano's cooperation contributed to the nation's welfare is still a military secret, but it certainly contributed to Luciano's welfare. He was paroled at the war's end and allowed to return to his native Italy, on condition that he never again set foot in the United States.

From exile Luciano continued to influence the syndicate, but active leadership passed to Joe Adonis, Frank Costello, and Meyer Lansky. Right after World War II, however, Lansky ran into a series of problems that kept him from enjoying his new prestige. First, his ally, Fulgencio Batista, failed to win the presidency in Cuba, and Lansky once more had to postpone his plans for developing Havana.

Second, his personal life became quite complicated. Right after the war, Lansky met Thelma Schwartz, a manicurist at a New York hotel, and decided to marry her. But first he had to persuade his wife, the former Anna Citron, to give him a divorce while allowing him the companionship of their two sons and one daughter.

Finally, Lansky's old friend Bugsy Siegel was causing trouble for the syndicate. He was spending too much of its money to build the Flamingo Hotel in Las Vegas. And he was ignoring advice and getting involved in a factional struggle within the underworld for control of the wire service that supplied bookies with racetrack information. In short, he was showing the kind of growing independence and recklessness that threatened the subtle organization that men like Lansky were building. So, early in 1947, syndicate leaders met in a Havana hotel suite with Lucky Luciano to decide what to do about Bugsy. Luciano had sneaked back from Italy hoping to re-enter the United States. What occurred is not known, but it is certain that Lansky, a man who would not hesitate to put the organization above loyalty to an old friend, went along with the decision reached at the meeting.

On June 20, 1947, Siegel was sitting in the Beverly Hills home of his mistress, Virginia Hill, when two steel-jacketed slugs from an Army carbine tore through the window and into his face. One bullet smashed the bridge of his nose and drove into his left eye. The other entered his right cheek, passed through the back of his neck and shattered a vertebra. His right eye was later discovered on the dining-room floor fifteen feet away.

The Flamingo Hotel, which had gotten Siegel into trouble, started paying dividends the very day Bugsy was shot. Lansky, one of the original twenty-one investors, got back many times over the $62,500 he had put up. So did other syndicate leaders. They went on to build bigger and better hotels and casinos and to make even more money, thanks to a large degree to the ill-fated Bugsy. For it was Siegel who had awakened them to the gold in Las Vegas years before, when all they could see there was sand. However, it did not help Bugsy at all in the end.

(The Flamingo later changed hands several times, but Lansky continued to follow the fortunes of the old place with keen interest, as his recent indictment demonstrates. In 1960, when the Parvin-Dohrmann Company of Los Angeles, which owned the Flamingo at the time, was trying to sell it, Lansky turned up once again. Parvin-Dohrmann, a distributor of hotel supplies and equipment, paid Lansky $200,000 as a finder's fee for helping in the sale of the hotel. "Flamingo recognizes and acknowledges that it has been solely through the information and advice supplied by Lansky that the sale may be made . . ." said a contract signed by Lansky and Albert Parvin, then head of the company, on May 12, 1960.)

Lansky worked feverishly to take advantage of the post-war boom by launching hundreds of new operations all over the country. He started real-estate companies in several states; set up juke-box-distribution outlets in Baltimore, Philadelphia, and New York; opened a string of new casinos that stretched from Miami, Florida, to Saratoga, New York; and bought into several television manufacturing and servicing companies. The money from all these ventures rolled in with such speed that even Lansky had difficulty counting it. Records show that two of his illegal casinos in Florida—Greenacres and La Boheme—brought in $1.6 million during one four-month period in 1949 alone.

Then in 1950 the Kefauver Committee turned the spotlight on Lansky, and America caught a glimpse of his power for the first time. The heat of the investigation forced officials in Florida and New York to shut down Lansky's casinos and to make noises about sending him to prison. He was indicted for gambling violations in both states and an effort was started to have him deported. But in the end he served only a three-month sentence in New York—the first and last time Lansky ever went to jail.

When he got out, he headed for Cuba to revive his old dream of turning Havana into a gambling paradise. His old friend Batista, who had won back the presidency in 1952 with syndicate financing, gave him free rein.

Lansky made Cuba a gambling monopoly for himself and selected syndicate friends. He had a law passed that allowed gambling only in hotels worth $1 million or more, and proceeded to build the only hotels that would qualify. To safe-guard his employees, he had Cuban immigration regulations adjusted so that his dealers, pit bosses, and stick men would be classified as "valuable technicians."

During this period the triumvirate that ruled the syndicate began to break up. First, Joe Adonis was deported to Italy; then Frank Costello was persuaded to retire, not because of old age or poor health but because of overexposure. He was too well known and too well identified with crime to remain the leader of the kind of organization the syndicate was becoming. (Shortly afterward Costello was replaced as head of his Mafia family as well. He did not protest either demotion and was allowed to go on living.)

As soon as he became a primary force in the underworld, Lansky began instituting a number of changes that enabled the syndicate to penetrate deep into the economic life of America. He curtailed the practice of buying up small companies through friends and relatives. Such men always turned out to be more loyal than competent, and the businesses never got very far. Instead, he started sending syndicate money to secret accounts in Europe, from which authorized middlemen would lend it to American executives in urgent need of capital. "Some of the biggest mergers and acquisitions in recent years have been financed with syndicate money from Europe," says a Securities and Exchange Commission official.

To represent the syndicate in the sophisticated businesses it was financing, Lansky began recruiting bright young men with no links to the underworld. He trains them in the art of being invisible, which he has perfected. These men will be the inheritors of power in organized crime, making the job of law enforcement officials in the future even more difficult than it is now. "At least the old bunch had records and we knew them," says one police official. "It will take us years just to identify this new button-down breed. And some we'll probably never know."

The admiration Lansky won for his innovations was slightly tarnished in 1959 when he lost Cuba to Fidel Castro. Lansky flew out of Havana on the same day that Batista did, but he left his brother Jake behind to see if he could arrange a deal with Castro's men. Not only did the Cuban revolutionaries refuse to play ball, but they kept Jake hostage for twenty-five days before letting him return to Florida.

Lansky was so angry that he called a meeting of the syndicate's board and persuaded it to put a $1 million price on Castro's head. It was partly this bounty that worried United States officials when Castro later visited New York for a United Nations session and refused to abide by security restrictions. But the concern was unnecessary. By that time Lansky had withdrawn the bounty. Never a man to live in the past, he had become resigned to losing Cuba and was already focusing on the Bahamas.

In 1963 a plush new hotel, the Lucayan Beach, was built in Freeport on Grand Bahama Island by

odox manner he has achieved his goal. He sees
syndicate as a huge corporation whose growth
profits depend on his efforts. The new gener-
 of syndicate members with Brooks Brothers
 and degrees in accounting looks to him for
ance. Henry Ford and Andrew Carnegie could
give up the risks and challenges of a lifetime
ty-five, and neither can Lansky.

e has spent most of his life trying to reach a
ion where he could play the big executive:
loping plans for vast new enterprises around
world, making decisions that involve millions.
has extorted, robbed, and murdered to get
e he is, and now he cannot give it all up
 though it means he can never enjoy his great
h as long as he goes on. Meyer Lansky, a vic-
er of men and laws for half a century, is him-
 victim of his own dream.

a group of companies under the control of Wallace
Groves, an ex-convict who had settled on the island twenty years previously. Just before the Lucayan Beach was finished, Groves got permission
from the Bahamian government to operate a casino in the hotel.

Soon after it opened, the casino was running
with an efficiency worthy of the best gambling
parlors controlled by Lansky in Las Vegas. And
with good reason. The men in charge turned out
to be three long-time Lansky associates—Max
Courtney, Frank Ritter, and Charles Brudner. Another key operative was Dan "Dusty" Peters, a
Lansky courier of long and loyal service, who was
observed making frequent trips to Miami Beach
for meetings with Lansky.

Then in 1966 it was revealed that some of the
highest officials in the United Bahamian party
had received secret payments from several companies controlled by Groves. Sir Stafford Sands,
then minister of finance and tourism, later acknowledged to a Commission of Inquiry that Lansky had offered him $2 million in 1960 to permit
gambling on Grand Bahama. Sands said he had
turned the gangster down. He insisted that the
$1.8 million he had received from Groves's com-
panies was for "consultant and legal fees."

These revelations toppled the United Bahamian party from power. Sands left the Bahamas
for a castle he owns in Spain, and Lansky's men

were expelled from the islands. Fear of Lansky's continued influence in the Bahamas has remained strong, however. When one of the new managers of the Lucayan Beach casino, Hyman Lazar, was observed fraternizing with Lansky in Miami Beach, the present operators of the casino quickly dismissed him.

With the heat on in the Bahamas, Lansky turned his attention to the growing number of casinos that were opening in England, Europe, and the Middle East. In England, for example, hundreds of small casinos and several large ones opened after Parliament in 1960 passed a law permitting gaming under certain conditions. It was hardly surprising that Lansky's man Dino Cellini should show up as manager of the Colony Club, a posh casino in London's Berkeley Square, after being kicked out of the Bahamas.

Cellini was followed by another of Lansky's old friends—George Raft. The actor's associations with underworld figures go back to his premovie days, when he worked as a beer runner for Owney "The Killer" Madden. His trip to Hollywood was financed by the mob, and it was he who introduced Bugsy Siegel to Hollywood society in the late 1930's. Over the years Raft has been a front for a travel agency in California and a supermarket in Arizona. He worked for Lansky at the El Casino de Capri in Havana, ostensibly as an entertainment director, until Castro closed the place.

Both Cellini and Raft were expelle[d] authorities, and the Colony Club wa[s] their departure in no way ended Lan[sky] in English casinos. He merely turned [to] fiable fronts recruited locally. At pres[ent] known to control at least five majo[r] England, mainland Europe, and the [Caribbean] —and to be shopping around for oth[ers] exile to Israel to avoid prosecution i[n the United] States has not meant that he is slowi[ng] the string of syndicate emissaries who [visit Tel] Aviv every month clearly demonstrates [that]

At an age when several of his ol[d friends in] crime are selling their interests in t[he syndicate,] setting up trusts for their children, [and being] grateful for the chance to die of n[atural causes,] Lansky is still scanning the world fo[r new frontiers] for syndicate activities. He has mor[e money than] he can use, and at present he has ve[ry little oppor]tunity to enjoy it. He has reached [the top of the] ladder unscathed, while the closest [friends of his] youth have been jailed, deported, [or killed in] gangland killings. Why doesn't he [relax] and retire?

The only answer that seems [plausible is] that he thrives on the challenge [of remain]ing in the vanguard of organize[d crime. His] former idol Bugsy Siegel alwa[ys wanted] to be a movie star, Lansky has [wanted to be] a powerful business executive.

4

JOE COLOMBO— MAFIA MAVERICK

ON JUNE 28, 1971, thousands of Italian-Americans milled around Manhattan's Columbus Circle in the shimmering heat waiting for the beginning of the Italian-American Civil Rights League's second annual Unity Day—a celebration of ethnic strength and solidarity.

Near the foot of the huge statue of Columbus, Joseph Colombo, Sr., forty-eight, the founder of the league and the man responsible for all the festivity, was greeting friends, shaking hands, posing for photographers. Less than fifteen minutes before noon, when the ceremony was officially to begin, a black man named Jerome Johnson came up behind Colombo and fired three shots into the back of his head and neck. Before the crowd could realize what had happened, another volley of shots rang out and Johnson lay dead in a pool of his own blood.

The bullets from Johnson's automatic abruptly interrupted one of the most fascinating careers in recent Mafia history. For Joseph Colombo symbolized to the public, to law enforcement officials, and to Mafiosi alike a new and modern kind of Mafia boss.

The Mafia has changed a great deal since the days of the peasant uprisings in sun-baked Sicily. It has found a place within its ranks for business-school graduates, and it has adopted modern banking methods and invested in legitimate corporate ventures. But Joseph Colombo, the youngest family boss in the Mafia, was the first to believe that he could effectively add to his arsenal such modern weapons as the public relations release, the press interview, and the civil rights demonstration, and the rest of the Mafia watched his progress with the greatest interest.

Five days after it had taken place the police labeled the shooting an underworld plot, perpetrated by "rivals of Colombo" in the "Italian underworld community" who hired Jerome Johnson to kill Colombo at the Columbus Circle rally. The police also suggested that the publicity Colombo had generated by founding the league had made certain Mafia figures unhappy and that Colombo was "in disfavor in the underworld."

It is surprising that Joe Colombo should have emerged as a rebellious leader who earned the enmity of the Mafia establishment because his background could not have been more conventional by Mafia standards. Indeed, during most of his career he seized every opportunity to ingratiate himself with the establishment. "He was the Mafia's Sammy Glick," said one police officer.

Before 1962 Joe Colombo was merely a soldier in the family then headed by Joseph Profaci. He inherited his association with the Profaci family from his father, Anthony Colombo, a mobster who in 1939 was found dead in his car next to the body of a woman friend. Both had been garroted. Underworld informants told police that Anthony Colombo had been killed for infringing Mafia rules. When a reporter once asked Joe Colombo if he had ever tried to discover the identity of his father's murderer he snapped, "Don't they pay policemen for that?"

Joe's big break in the Mafia came in 1962, when Joseph Bonanno, the leader of a New York family and a member of the Mafia's national commission, got ambitious and decided to try to become the dominant force in the Mafia. Bonanno's plan called for killing Mafia leaders Carlo Gambino and Thomas Luchese, both of New

York, and Stefano Magaddino of Buffalo. He gave the contracts for the assassinations to his colleague Giuseppe Magliocco, who had succeeded Profaci. Magliocco in turn farmed out the killings to Joe Colombo, a newly appointed *capo* in his family. According to underword sources, Joe decided that the intended victims could do him more good than Bonanno, so instead of carrying out the contracts, he told Gambino about the projected coup. Bonanno ultimately was forced to surrender leadership of his family and moved to Arizona. Magliocco repented of his part in the scheme, was fined, and died shortly afterward.

The leadership of Magliocco's family and his seat on the commission went to Joe Colombo, apparently as a reward for exposing Bonanno's plans. When Joe took over the family in 1964, he sidelined most of the old guard then in power and replaced them with the younger men pressing for position. His meteoric rise was frequently discussed inside the Mafia.

It was a topic, for example, in the taped conversations of reputed New Jersey Mafia leader Simone Rizzo "Sam the Plumber" DeCavalcante that were released by the FBI on a federal court order in 1969. Sam was talking to his underboss, Frank Majuri. Here is part of the exchange:

DE CAVALCANTE: This guy [Colombo] sits like a baby next to Carl [Gambino] all the time. He'd do anything Carl wants him to do. . . .

MAJURI: So who the hell are you going to trust?

DE CAVALCANTE: See, this kid is inexperienced. . . .

MAJURI: I told you, Sam, I was surprised when I heard he was in there [head of the Brooklyn family]. I would never have made that guess.

DE CAVALCANTE: What experience has he got? He was a bustout guy [petty gambler] all his life. . . . What does he know?

The Mafia family Joe Colombo came to dominate differed in many ways from other families in New York, according to law enforcement officials. With approximately 220 members and associates, it was small in size compared, say, to the Carlo Gambino family, which is believed to be four times as big.

Federal, state, and city agents who followed the activities of Joe's family believed that it represented the "new look" in the Mafia. "Most of its members are American-born, free-wheeling men not so bound to tradition and eager to find new ways to exploit the system," said a federal agent.

The Colombo family rackets were located almost exclusively in Brooklyn and Long Island, whereas the interests of several of the other families are spread all the way from New Haven to the outskirts of Philadelphia. The rackets of the family included numbers and sports gambling, hijacking, fencing in stolen goods, and loan-sharking (lending money at usurious interest).

Unlike some older family bosses, Colombo concentrated on getting his men involved in legitimate business to help justify their expenditures. "It was almost a fetish with him," said an FBI agent. Colombo himself worked as a salesman for the Cantalupo Realty Company in Brooklyn.

Before going to work for Cantalupo early in the 1960's, he was employed for six years as a salesman for the Pride Wholesale Meat Company, which was controlled by Peter Castellano and Paul Gambino, brother of Carlo Gambino. Castellano was a captain in the Gambino family. For ten years before joining the meat company, Colombo worked intermittently as a longshoreman, according to information he once volunteered to a credit investigator. Before that he spent three years in the Coast Guard, being discharged for medical reasons.

After Colombo began working for Cantalupo Realty, he liked to boast about his prowess as a salesman. In 1970, when the New York State Legislative Committee on Crime questioned Anthony A. Cantalupo, president of the company, about his famous salesman, Cantalupo said that he considered Colombo "a perfect gentleman." He added that Colombo had "the sincerest group of clients—they don't cheat him out of his commissions."

A small, squarely built, muscular man, Colombo liked shoulder pads, wide ties, and diamond cuff links, and he kept his expensive Italian-made shoes brilliantly shined. By the time he was shot his square jaw had been somewhat obscured by heavy jowls, his dark hair was receding, and his eyes seemed as narrow as slits because of the puffiness of the flesh beneath them. But his manner commanded respect.

Home to Colombo and his platinum-blonde wife, Lucille, was a split-level house in the Bensonhurst section of Brooklyn. The youngest of their four sons and their little daughter lived with them. The house, which Colombo had built in 1962, sat on a small hill behind a wide driveway that led to an underground garage.

The Colombos also owned a more imposing estate at Blooming Grove, New York. Amenities there are reported to have included tennis courts, a handball court, stables, and a swimming pool.

The estate was assessed in 1966 at $86,200.

Early in 1970, after his son, Joseph, Jr., was arrested by the FBI on charges of conspiring to melt silver coins into more valuable ingots, Joseph Colombo, Sr., took a step that dramatically set him apart from all the Mafia bosses who had preceded him. He founded the Italian-American Civil

Rights League in order, he said, to fight "a conspiracy against all Italian-Americans." The league believes that law enforcement officials and the media, by the use of words like "Mafia," have created the false impression that organized crime in the United States is made up only of gangsters of Italian descent. Another of Colombo's sons, Anthony, was vice president of the league at a weekly salary of $300. (Joe, Jr., was acquitted early in 1971 after a key government witness suddenly recanted his testimony.)

The league received widespread support from thousands of Italian-Americans with no underworld connections but with a strong sense of ethnic injustice. The league's successes began to make news. Its members picketed the FBI offices in Manhattan for months on end. It succeeded in having the words "Mafia" and "Cosa Nostra" eliminated from several newspapers, most television shows, and all Justice Department releases. (During the week that the league was picketing the Staten Island *Advance,* a truck loaded with copies of the newspaper was burned, and its two drivers were beaten with tire irons. According to league spokesmen, either it did not happen or "they did it to themselves.")

On Columbus Day, 1970, the league staged a rally of Italian-Americans at Columbus Circle in New York City. Some fifty thousand people, including the entire Gambino family, crowded the streets. New York's waterfront was shut down so that longshoremen could take the day off with pay to attend, and nearly every important New York City politician showed up.

Elation ran high and Joe Colombo was in his element, making speeches before the television cameras and kissing babies. He told the crowd: "I say there is a conspiracy against me, against all Italian-Americans. I believe Nixon is behind it. But you and Joe Colombo are together today under God's eyes . . . and those who get in our way will feel His sting."

In retrospect it is not hard to see that first Columbus Circle rally as the first act in a Greek tragedy. Undoubtedly the seeds of hubris took root in Colombo's mind when he saw fifty thousand of his fellow Italian-Americans cheering him as the patriarch of their community. In the face of such adulation it was easy to forget propriety, discretion, and the ancient Mafia tradition of *omertà* (silence). When, exactly one year later, Colombo's blood stained the pavement near the foot of the statue of Columbus, which had been draped in the red, green, and white plastic bunting of the league, the outcome of the tragedy seemed almost Aristotelian in its symmetry.

Joe's attempts to create a good image for himself and the league were not 100 per cent successful at first. His physical appearance, his gravelly voice, and the sinister presence of glowering muscle men at every press conference reminded the public of a popular stereotype of a gangster. But Colombo learned some sophistication in dealing with the media. He agreed to give interviews to carefully selected reporters, but he firmly refused to talk to reporters, including me, who because of their past writing and background might ask uncomfortable questions.

Whenever a reporter asked Joe about his ties with the underworld or his criminal record (when he was shot he was appealing a conviction for perjury and was under two indictments, including one charging him with heading a vast gambling operation in Brooklyn), he usually launched into rhetoric about a "conspiracy of discrimination" and ethnic slurs.

Joe's emergence as a star of television, radio, and the press, and his efforts on behalf of the Italian-American community, did not endear him to other Mafiosi, however. "You hear more criticism than compliments in the Mafia about Joe these days," said a federal agent who had monitored telephone conversations between organized crime figures early in 1971.

Even some members of Colombo's own Mafia family were grumbling. They complained that Colombo's well-publicized attacks on the FBI and other law enforcement agencies made all family members—20 per cent of whom were under indictment for various infractions by the summer of

1971—targets of lawmen. "You do a favor for Joe these days and you wind up in trouble," said one member of the family to a lawman in April, 1971.

The FBI denied focusing special attention on any particular group of criminals, but they acknowledged that they had greater success in organized crime cases in general after the league's demonstrations started. "When you have to walk through a picket line to get to the office, you tend to work a lot harder," one agent said.

Grumbling about Colombo was also heard from members of other families who felt that his antics were focusing undue attention on the Mafia. They complained, in addition, that Colombo had the league stage demonstrations whenever he or his son was arrested but that he showed little interest when other Mafia figures were in the same predicament.

The only leader of organized crime who consistently backed Colombo in the early days of the league was his old benefactor Carlo Gambino, whose life he had saved by revealing Bonanno's assassination plans. But Gambino, who came to the United States as a stowaway in 1921 when he was nineteen, was a cautious man who had risen to the leadership of one of the largest Mafia families in the country by operating quietly and subtly, and in time he was bound to find Colombo's tactics unsettling.

Colombo, however, worried mostly about opponents within his own family. Friction in the family dated back to the early 1960's, when the family, not yet under Colombo's rule, had been torn by an internal conflict known as the Profaci-Gallo war. The family was then led by Joseph Profaci, a powerful Mafioso who owned a 328-acre estate with its own airport in Hightown, New York. In 1960 a dissident group within the family, led by the notorious brothers Larry, Joseph, and Albert Gallo, began kidnapping Profaci lieutenants in a dispute with Profaci over illegal profits. Profaci died of cancer in 1962, but the war continued under his successor Giuseppe Magliocco.

The conflict finally petered out, leaving at least a dozen gangsters dead, when a powerful ally of the Gallos, Tony Bender, suddenly disappeared, Joe Gallo was sent to prison for extortion, and Larry was stricken with cancer. Thus Albert, the least effective of the three brothers, was left in charge of the Gallo faction of the family.

On March 10, 1971, Joseph Gallo, forty-two, was released from prison. Soon afterward he began to complain that his faction was still being ill-treated by the family and that Colombo's involvement in the league was hurting the Mafia. During his nine years in prison Joe Gallo, who earned his nickname of "Crazy Joe" when court psychiatrists at a 1947 trial said he suffered from paranoia, had developed strong friendships with black convicts and had reportedly sent some of them upon their release to South Brooklyn, where his gang helped them to find jobs.

In addition to Gallo, such powerful figures in the family as Carmine "The Snake" Persico strongly criticized Colombo's tactics. Persico, who commanded a strong faction in the family, was not as blatant in his attacks as Crazy Joe, and on the surface he maintained a cordial relationship with Colombo. At the same time, however, he seized every opportunity to point out that the fortunes of the family had declined markedly under Colombo's leadership.

Before the Unity Day shooting, Joe Colombo was well aware that he was in trouble with many of his fellow Mafiosi. Members of the Gallo gang reportedly warned a number of merchants in their South Brooklyn turf not to close on Unity Day. Posters put up by the league abruptly disappeared from walls. Rumors floated through the underworld that Colombo men had extorted large sums of money from merchants on the pretense that they were raising it for the league.

The one man who could have averted the impending violence was Carlo Gambino. Colombo had been his protégé, and Gambino and his gang had supported the first Unity Day in 1970. But as the second annual Unity Day approached, key Gambino men began resigning from the league. Longshoremen on the waterfront, part of Gambino's empire, were told that, unlike 1970, they would not have Unity Day off with pay. The withdrawal of support by Gambino, the oldest and most powerful Mafia leader in New York, made it clear that the Mafia establishment was fed up with Joe Colombo. And that meant that the establishment was not likely to object to any action being taken against the maverick Mafioso.

Despite a noticeable cooling of enthusiasm among his underworld associates, Joe Colombo continued to devote his full energy to the preparations for Unity Day. Some considered his obsession with the rally to be foolhardy to the point of madness. But Joe was never one to view things rationally. According to his Coast Guard record, he was sentenced to a year's confinement for going absent without leave three times but received a medical discharge before completing the sentence because he suffered from "psychoneurosis." The medical report in his record says that he was "unable to adapt to the restrictions of military life because of tension and instability...."

While Joe's supporters girded themselves for Unity Day and worried about the uneasy stirring of his opponents, Colombo predicted a record turnout for the rally, estimating that it would be as high as half a million people. When he was cut down by Johnson's bullets, there were only about twenty thousand people at Columbus Circle. Afterward the horrified crowd waited for reports of Joe's condition as the speeches went on in a desultory fashion. Several black men unlucky enough to be on the scene were roughed up.

But when the crowd finally started to wend its way home in the hot sun, it was clear that Joe's experiment in removing the Mafia from the minds and lips of America had failed. The moment the bullet slammed into his head, the word "Mafia" once again took on its most sinister meaning.

Joe also failed in his bold attempt to update the image of the modern Mafia boss. In the intoxicating blaze of publicity which made him a superstar he had forgotten one basic fact that distinguishes the Mafia from legitimate corporations. No matter how promising a young man may seem, no matter how great his personal fame and public following may become, the Mafia is an illegal operation that depends for its life on anonymity. And the Mafia, unlike any other conglomerate, has one very effective weapon for enforcing its rules and traditions: it shoots people.

5

FRANK SINATRA— FRIENDS FOREVER

"FRIENDSHIP IS EVERYTHING," says the Mafia don in Mario Puzo's novel *The Godfather*. "Friendship is more than talent. It is more than government. It is almost the equal of family. Never forget that."

The Mafia leader addresses this advice to a character named Johnny Fontane, an Italian singer who revives his sagging career with a straight acting role. Many readers consider the career change to be one of the numerous similarities between the fictitious Johnny Fontane and singer

Frank Sinatra, who revived his career in 1953 with his Academy Award-winning performance in *From Here to Eternity*. (The successful comeback allowed Sinatra to announce his retirement early in 1971 while at the top of his profession.)

But those who know Sinatra well would realize that the similarity between Johnny Fontane and Frank Sinatra is superficial. Frank Sinatra, for instance, would not need the lecture on friendship from the Mafia don. For Sinatra has, for thirty years, honored his friendships with Mafia leaders even though they have tarnished his image, damaged his business interests, and cost him his amiable relationship with the late President John F. Kennedy.

It is not at all unusual for singers to have to deal with gangsters, who have a stake in many of the nightclubs where entertainers get their start. But no other entertainer has ever built such acquaintances into enduring friendships. Although Sinatra has never been accused of participating in any illegal Mafia enterprises, he has visited the homes of Mafiosi, introduced them to women, and apparently allowed them to use his name to try to win favors from government officials.

Even at the peak of his fame, Sinatra did not hesitate to fly to Cuba to pay his respects to the exiled Mafia boss Lucky Luciano, nor, on the eve of appearing at a New York rally to improve the image of Italians in America, did he neglect to visit the nearby home of Dave Iacovetti, a major East Coast Mafia figure.

Sinatra did not limit his friendships with gangsters even after they shattered his carefully constructed contacts with John F. Kennedy. When Kennedy won the Democratic presidential nomination in 1960, the singer raised money for the young Senator, joined him on campaign trips, and praised him to everyone who would listen.

When Kennedy was elected, Sinatra redoubled his efforts and devoted ten exhausting weeks to planning a gala party in Washington for the eve of the inauguration. Tickets cost $100 to $10,000, and Sinatra's efforts erased $1.4 million of campaign debts in a single night.

The extravaganza, which featured performers ranging from Jimmy Durante to Sir Laurence Olivier, was an unforgettable "opening night" for the glamour of the Kennedy years. No one doubted that Sinatra would be the favored entertainer at the White House. But after a time things began to sour.

The singer's relations with the President began to deteriorate after Robert Kennedy took office as Attorney General and launched a campaign against organized crime in the United States. Before long, veteran investigators at the Justice Department complained that they did not understand how the administration could both wage war on the Mafia and welcome at the White House a man as closely tied to Mafia leaders as Frank Sinatra.

Robert Kennedy ordered the organized crime section at the Justice Department to give him a report on Sinatra's Mafia associations. Although the department had never investigated Sinatra himself, surveillance of many of the leading gangsters in the country had produced indications of a relationship between the gangsters and the entertainer, and a Justice lawyer was set to work compiling all the scattered information into one special report.

After studying the Justice Department report, Robert Kennedy felt it was significant enough to take to his brother. While President Kennedy was examining it, an incident took place that fueled the fire.

A friend of Sinatra's—Sam "Moe" Giancana, a leader of the Mafia in Chicago—became irked at the continual close surveillance of FBI agents. He sent an aide to tell the agents that he, Giancana, wanted to confer with Robert Kennedy himself about ending the surveillance. As for the mechanics of setting up such a high-level meeting, the aide told the agents: "Moe says that if Kennedy wants to talk, he should get in touch with Frank Sinatra to set it up."

According to one of Robert Kennedy's assistants, the Attorney General not only disregarded the invitation but took the FBI report of the incident to the President.

The honeymoon between the President and Frank Sinatra was over. This became all too clear when JFK visited Palm Springs and stayed at the home of Bing Crosby. The special wing that Sinatra had added to his Palm Springs home, in anticipation of President Kennedy's visits, was to remain unoccupied.

Sinatra soon learned from friends in the Kennedy circle that it was Bobby Kennedy who had persuaded the President to break with him, and the singer never forgave him. As his mother once said of Sinatra, "My son is like me. You cross him, he never forgets." Peter Lawford, the President's brother-in-law, was no longer a welcome member of Sinatra's court. And no one who knew the singer well was at all surprised when, in 1968, he announced his support for Hubert Humphrey for the Democratic presidential nomination soon after Robert Kennedy declared that he would be a candidate. "Bobby's just not qualified to be President," Sinatra said.

There has been much speculation as to the contents of the Justice Department report on Frank Sinatra. As standard procedure, the department will not reveal its contents or even acknowledge that such a report exists. However, I have been able to secure a copy of the report through special sources.

It is a nineteen-page document dated August 3, 1962, and titled "Francis Albert Sinatra, a/k/a Frank Sinatra." The information in it is based partly on the reports of FBI agents who followed gangsters associated with Sinatra and monitored their telephone conversations, and partly on information supplied by government informants, who are identified by code names like "LA T-79."

The report establishes the fact that Sinatra was in contact with about ten of the best-known gangsters in the country in the late 1950's and early 1960's. It details exact dates when some of these gangsters telephoned Sinatra's home, using his unlisted number, and it enumerates special favors that Sinatra performed for some of them.

One of these favors involved a car dealer named Peter Epsteen. He tried to persuade Sinatra to record a singing commercial for his Pontiac agency in Skokie, Illinois, but the singer refused. Then Epsteen brought the matter to the attention of Joseph and Rocco Fischetti, cousins of Al Capone and leading Mafia figures, "after which Sinatra made the commercial as a favor without charge," the report quotes Epsteen's former wife as telling FBI agents. (Sinatra did, however, agree to accept two Pontiacs as a gift from the grateful Epsteen, the report adds.)

Spokesmen for Sinatra later said that the commercial was done as a personal favor to Epsteen and had nothing to do with the Fischetti brothers. But the Justice Department report does point out that after the commercial was made, Joseph Fischetti and a close lady friend of Rocco Fischetti's were seen driving Pontiacs "bearing Epsteen's dealer's license plate and label."

Sinatra's favors to the Fischetti brothers went beyond his willingness to sing a commercial for their friend. The Justice Department report indicates that Sinatra arranged for Joe Fischetti to receive payments as a talent scout from the Fontainebleau Hotel in Miami Beach whenever Sinatra performed at the hotel.

The report quotes an informant as saying that as of April, 1962, "Joe Fischetti, under the name of Joe Fisher, had received 71 checks from the Fontainebleau Hotel, each in the amount of $540.00 (Total: $38,340.00)." It is difficult to double-check such a statement, but the report does point out that Joe Fischetti, in his income tax returns from 1959 and 1960, listed fees of $12,960 from the Fontainebleau Hotel as a "talent agent."

The report adds that in Miami Beach "Fischetti is Sinatra." It says that Sinatra usually entertained there for a contract price plus a cash deal and that the cash deal was generally handled by Fischetti. The report also says that Sinatra reportedly lent Fischetti $90,000 to help the gangster buy a secret interest in a large Miami restaurant.

Sinatra's favors to his gangster friends have not been solely of a financial nature. The report indicates that sometime in 1961 a twenty-eight-year-old divorcée acquaintance of Sinatra's was introduced to Chicago mobster Sam Giancana, the man who later complained about the FBI agents tailing him. Giancana, a short, bald man with a harmless-looking smile and a mild manner, was rejected by his draft board in 1944 as a psychopath. At fifteen he was sent to jail for auto theft, and by the time he was twenty he had been questioned in connection with three murders.

Giancana does not look like a Don Juan, but he has an eye for beautiful women. He has been widely seen and photographed in the company of Phyllis McGuire, of the singing McGuire sisters. He was so pleased with the companionship of the young divorcée to whom Sinatra introduced him that he showered her with expensive gifts, including a new Thunderbird sports car.

The Justice Department report also indicates that Sinatra may have been involved with gangsters in business dealings in Nevada. Early in the 1960's he owned a controlling interest in the Cal-Neva Lodge, a resort complex and casino on Nevada's beautiful Lake Tahoe. The report quotes Sam Giancana as bragging to friends that he owned a piece of Cal-Neva through Sinatra.

While the singer owned the lodge, he employed Paul Emilio D'Amato, a New Jersey underworld figure, as an overseer. The report says that D'Amato's actual purpose was to protect Giancana's interest in the lodge.

The Cal-Neva Lodge was the setting for some dramatic encounters in Sinatra's life. The Justice Department report says that in the summer of 1962 the singer made "improper advances" to a cocktail waitress at the lodge who happened to be married to a local deputy sheriff. The lawman warned Sinatra to leave his wife alone, the report says, but the singer persisted in his advances. On or about June 30, 1962, the angry deputy sheriff walked up to Sinatra in the casino and punched him in the face so hard that he had to cancel his singing engagement.

The bruises healed, but a year later Sinatra ran into real trouble at the lodge. The cause of it was his powerful friend from Chicago, Sam Giancana, who arrived at the Cal-Neva with his traveling companion, singer Phyllis McGuire.

Giancana was missed by his faithful shadows in Chicago, and the State Gaming Control Board in Nevada soon traced him, through informants, to Chalet 50 of the Cal-Neva Lodge. Giancana happened to be one of eleven gangsters on the gaming board's blacklist—a black folder circulated to all casinos with the names, pictures, and backgrounds of the men considered *personae non grata* in the state.

The gaming board had warned that if any of the gangsters on the blacklist were allowed into any casino, its license would be revoked. Therefore, when Giancana was traced to Cal-Neva, the chairman of the gaming board, Edward A. Olsen, called Frank Sinatra to his office for an explanation.

Olsen says that Sinatra admitted having seen Giancana at the lodge, but denied having invited him there. He promised not to associate with the gang leader in Nevada anymore, but said that Giancana was a friend and that if he wanted to see him outside the state, it was his own business.

Olsen says he replied that as long as Sinatra associated with gangsters at all while holding an interest in Nevada casinos, it reflected badly on gambling in the state. But Sinatra refused to yield, Olsen says, and the gaming board began to amass evidence to file a complaint against the entertainer.

Several days after the meeting with the singer, according to Olsen, Sinatra telephoned him at his office and invited him to Cal-Neva for dinner "to talk about this thing." Olsen replied that he did not think such a visit appropriate, since the board was investigating the lodge. "But he kept insisting," Olsen says, "and I kept refusing. The more I refused the madder he got, until he seemed almost hysterical. He used the foulest language I ever heard in my life."

Finally, Olsen says, Sinatra declared that if his invitation was refused, he would never talk to anyone from the board. Olsen says he was angry himself by this time and told Sinatra that if the board wanted to talk to him, it would subpoena him.

"You subpoena me," Olsen quotes Sinatra as replying, "and you're going to get a big, fat, fucking surprise."

"It was clear to me he meant that as a threat," says Olsen.

The gaming board never subpoenaed Sinatra, but not because of the threat. After the board initiated formal proceedings to revoke his gaming license, the entertainer turned it in voluntarily and promised to sell his Nevada gambling interests, worth $3.5 million.

Before events reached that stage, however, gaming board officials and Nevada's Governor Grant Sawyer were subjected to pressures of a different kind. Paul D'Amato, Sinatra's right-hand man at Cal-Neva, tried to slip two $100 bills to gaming board agents who were making a routine inspection of the lodge. The agents returned the money and reported the offer.

Then Governor Sawyer got several phone calls from people who spoke about making large contributions to his upcoming campaign while at the same time discussing the Sinatra problem. "I told them that the rules were made for everyone, including Mr. Sinatra," he says. (Sawyer, who served two terms as governor, lost the election and is now practicing law in Las Vegas.)

Sinatra's involvement in Las Vegas ended in 1963, although he continued to appear as an entertainer there. But his involvement with underworld figures has persisted unabated despite the adverse publicity he has received and the financial losses he has suffered as a result of it. In 1963, Sinatra and singer Dean Martin turned up as directors of the Berkshire racetrack in Massachusetts. No one thought much about it until it was discovered some time later that Raymond Patriarca, the Mafia boss in New England, and Thomas "Three Finger Brown" Luchese, the late head of one of the five Mafia families in New York, had secret interests in the track.

In 1967 Sinatra performed at a big rally given in Madison Square Garden by the American-Italian Anti-Defamation League. However, in view of his underworld contacts, the choice of Sinatra to head a movement to improve the image of Italians in the United States shocked everyone. "The American-Italian Anti-Defamation League, in picking Frank Sinatra as their national leader, has chosen to add fire to fire," said *The New York Times* in an editorial. Before long, Sinatra resigned from the league. (Later, when Joe Colombo founded the Italian-American Civil Rights League in 1970, Sinatra gave it his full support.)

In 1968 Sinatra tried to make a political comeback in the Democratic party. He joined the campaign drive of presidential contender Hubert Humphrey and scheduled a series of fund-raising concerts for his benefit. But a *Wall Street Journal* article enumerating some of the singer's underworld contacts moved Humphrey to quietly cut him out of his campaign. (The dismissal, added to the treatment he had received under the Kennedys, soured Sinatra on many Democrats, and in 1970 he supported Republican Ronald Reagan for re-election as governor of California.)

In 1969 Sinatra's name was linked to several more gangsters. A Mafia figure named Angelo "Gyp" De Carlo was put on trial in New Jersey on charges of extortion. The FBI released some twenty-one thousand pages of recorded conversation De Carlo had had with other Mafiosi, and Sinatra's name figured on several of these pages. At one point a loan shark claimed that he would get money from Sinatra to buy a hotel in Jamaica. At another, De Carlo, whose sister-in-law is married to a cousin of Sinatra's, described an incident involving a woman Sinatra apparently wanted to see: "Russo says that while in Miami, Tony Bennett came over to the Racquet Club and says he's looking for this broad," De Carlo related. "I says, 'What do you want?'

"He says he wants this job [girl].

"I says, 'What are you talking about? Frank Sinatra sent a telegram wantin' this broad.' She was a beautiful thing, a real job.

"I called her up. I told her . . . [about] the telegram. It was a request by Frank for her to come to the coast, his telephone and all. I told her, 'Call him. Tell him to wire the money and go out there.' "

The De Carlo conversations were publicized at the same time that Sinatra was trying to avoid appearing before the New Jersey State Commission of Investigation, which had been looking into organized crime in that state, and the impact of the two events seriously hurt the singer's reputation. When he finally appeared before the commission, however, the furor had subsided.

Whether De Carlo really knew Sinatra or was just bragging (a frailty not uncommon among second-string Mafiosi) is uncertain. But it is clear that Frank Sinatra has long had relationships with a number of gangsters in his native New Jersey.

When he left his Hoboken home to pursue his dream of becoming a singer, performing for practically nothing in local roadhouses and clubs, he became fast friends with Quarico "Willie Moore" Moretti, a leader of the Mafia in New Jersey who, before his violent death, was involved in extortion, dope pushing, and murder.

While singing with Harry James's band in 1939, Sinatra made his first hit recording: "All or Nothing at All." When band leader Tommy Dorsey offered him $125 a week to be his vocalist, it seemed like a princely sum to Sinatra and he took the job. But his star continued to shoot upward, and crowds of bobbysoxers followed him everywhere.

The contract he had signed with Dorsey was shackling him. He could not take full advantage of his new-found fame. Suddenly and inexplicably the contract was canceled and Sinatra was a free agent. Dorsey never explained why he let such a valuable property go, but the story, much repeated among the underworld, was that Willie Moretti showed up at Dorsey's dressing room one night, put a gun into the band leader's mouth, and suggested that he sell Sinatra's contract. The price was one dollar.

Moretti continued to take a paternal interest in Sinatra, and eleven years later when the gossip columns were full of the news that the singer was going to divorce his first wife, Nancy, and marry Ava Gardner, the gangster fired off a telegram of advice to Sinatra: "I am very much surprised what I have been reading in the newspapers between you and your darling wife," Moretti wrote. "Remember you have a decent wife and children.

You should be very happy. Regards to all. Willie Moore."

Shortly thereafter, Moretti, his mental health weakened by advanced syphilis, was shot to death by fellow Mafiosi, who feared that he would talk.

Sinatra may have reflected on the fate of his old friend with some trepidation, but long before this his contacts with the underworld had reached to the very top of the Mafia ladder—namely to Salvatore Luciana, the Mafia boss who was better known as Lucky Luciano. Luciano was deported to Italy after World War II and spent his final years in Naples, but he did not give up his influence in Mafia affairs, even in exile. During one of his absences from home, Italian police found in Luciano's Naples apartment a gold cigarette case with this inscription: "To my dear pal Lucky, from his friend, Frank Sinatra."

In 1947 Luciano flew to Cuba from Naples in the vain hope to finding some way to get back into the United States. The arrival of the Mafia boss, only ninety miles from the United States, was such an important occasion in the underworld that thirty-six hotel suites were required to accommodate all the important gangsters who came to Havana to pay their respects. And along with the gangsters came Frank Sinatra to pay his respects to his "dear pal Lucky."

On the same plane with Sinatra were Joseph and Rocco Fischetti, the cousins of Al Capone.

Federal investigators later claimed that Rocco carried a bag with $2 million in "very large bills" to Luciano as part of his dividends from United States rackets.

The tremendous publicity generated by Sinatra's visit to Luciano moved the singer to offer an explanation: "I was brought up to shake a man's hand when I am introduced to him without first investigating his past," he said. Luciano's past, however, was not much of a secret, and the adverse publicity continued at such a pitch that Sinatra tried again to explain his presence in Cuba. He said he had run into one of the Fischetti brothers in Miami and mentioned that he was planning to make a little trip to Havana. The Fischetti brothers had also made plans to go to Havana and changed their reservations so they could fly down on the same plane with Sinatra.

When he got to Havana, Sinatra said, he was introduced to a large group of people who asked him to join them for dinner. And when he arrived at the dinner he discovered that Lucky Luciano was a guest as well. "It suddenly struck me that I was laying myself open to criticism by remaining at the table," Sinatra told the press, "but I could think of no way to leave in the middle of dinner without creating a scene."

In spite of his explanations, United States investigators learned from informers in the city that Sinatra did not just have dinner with Luciano and his friends, but spent four days with them, gambling and partying until the early morning hours. The only periods when Sinatra was not with the gangsters were when they held "business" meetings.

Sinatra continued to keep in touch with Luciano after the 1947 meeting, and he cultivated his association with the Fischetti brothers. Often when visiting Chicago the singer was seen paying a call at the home of Rocco Fischetti (who has since died), and whenever he was in Florida his entourage always included Joseph Fischetti, who became one of his most devoted associates.

The comments of a man who has often been part of Sinatra's entourage reveal just how close the singer's friendship with Joseph Fischetti became. "Frank is very touchy about his baldness and tells everyone to leave when he's going to change hair pieces," the man told me. "But if Joe Fischetti wants to stay, he stays."

A spokesman for Sinatra once berated a reporter who asked to interview the singer about his underworld contacts. "These reports are rumors and vicious, unnecessary attacks," the spokesman said. "Mr. Sinatra has associated with presidents, heads of state, and hundreds of personalities much more interesting and copyworthy. Why don't you write about those associations?"

It is precisely because of such associations that Sinatra's contacts with gangsters affect American society, suggests Ralph Salerno, a specialist on organized crime formerly with the New York Police Department. "People say to themselves, 'If Frank Sinatra, who knows presidents and kings, is friendly with Joe Fischetti, Sam Giancana, and all the rest, they can't be all that bad.' That's the service Sinatra renders his gangster friends. He gives them innocence by association. You'd think a guy like Sinatra would care about that. But he doesn't. He doesn't give a damn."

6

THE MAFIA
IS FULL
OF MALE
CHAUVINISTS

THE MAFIA is the surest stronghold of male chauvinism in America.

In the Mafia a woman may be a means to a profitable alliance with another Mafia "family"; a showcase for displaying her husband's wealth, status, and power; a valuable piece of property; a loyal helpmate; a good cook; a showy and ego-boosting mistress. But what she must never be is a liberated woman.

Joseph Valachi, the Mafioso who turned informer, made clear the degree to which a woman is considered a piece of property. He testified that two offenses bring the death penalty in the Mafia: "talking about the Cosa Nostra or violating another member's wife."

To an outsider the life of a Mafia wife, mistress, or daughter might seem to be surrounded by an aura of glamour. There is the constant threat of violence, the profusion of big money, stolen jewels, and furs, the thrill of belonging to a man who faces danger every day. Unfortunately the reality is a good deal drearier.

Only rarely do tales of wife-beatings, nervous breakdowns, suicides, and even the occasional murders of Mafia wives leak through the tight security of the underworld. But in spite of the all-important law of silence—the first law every Mafia woman learns—reports of the misery of Mafia women sometimes reach the outside world through wiretaps, informers' stories, court battles, and even occasionally through the desperate actions of the women themselves.

Mafia women responsible for major infractions of the rules have been killed or have had relatives or friends killed as punishment. Joseph Valachi told federal officials of one case in which a Mafia wife had had a brief liaison with a lesbian during a long absence of her husband. When the husband returned and found out what had happened, he could not bring himself to kill his wife; he took his revenge instead by having one of her friends shot to death. The friend's only crime was that he owned the club where the two women had met.

The social life of a Mafia wife is usually dull and restricted. When mobsters gather at the bars, casinos, nightclubs, restaurants, and racetracks where they do business, they would never dream of bringing their wives. The Mafia women live lives of inconspicuous luxury in homes that are clustered in certain neighborhoods of highly respectable suburbs.

Mafia wives are expected to limit their friendships to other Mafia wives. (To most of them this seems natural, since they are often related.) They keep busy with a constant round of weddings, baptisms, funerals, church functions, and charities. Some, however, occasionally rebel against such restrictions. Once the wife of a leading gangster called me in tears. The day before, a newspaper story of mine had appeared in which the address of her husband's $150,000 Manhattan townhouse was mentioned. Now, she said, two men were standing outside on the sidewalk surveying her house, and she was afraid of the effect the publicity might have on her children. I inquired gently why she did not live at Sands Point, Long Island, a fashionable suburb where there was a considerable settlement of Mafia homes. "Who wants to live out there," the woman exploded, "with all those creeps?"

Although she may have nearly unlimited money

available to her, a Mafia wife cannot spend it on things that will show. The Internal Revenue Service is constantly on the alert for expenditures by known or suspected Mafia members that seem out of line with the "legitimate" income that they report on their income tax forms. So, excessively palatial homes, extravagant cars, jewels, fur coats, and designer clothes bought through legitimate stores are all taboo for the Mafia woman.

As one sympathetic friend remarked about Joseph Colombo's platinum-blonde wife at the $125-a-plate testimonial dinner held for him in March, 1971, by the Italian-American Civil Rights League, "Poor Lucille has to walk around in rags because of those IRS jerks." (Nevertheless, "poor Lucille" and her family have two luxurious homes, one in Bensonhurst, Brooklyn, and another in Blooming Grove, New York. The latter includes tennis courts, stables, and a swimming pool.)

Not only must a Mafia wife spend money with one eye on the IRS, but she must be very careful to observe internal protocol. A Mafia family (*borgata*) is headed by a *capo famiglia*. Under him are an underboss and a *consigliere*. Next in line come a number of *capos,* who are each responsible for a certain number of soldiers. And a woman must be sure never to have a more expensive dress or car or house than her husband's superior or his wife.

to New York. One day Constance confronted him on a Brooklyn street and fired several bullets at him, hitting him twice but not wounding him seriously.

Rastelli, not surprisingly, refused to go back to her after that, and she threatened to talk to the authorities about him and his friends. At that point, she later told officials, she was visited by John "Big John" Ormento, a leading Mafioso who warned her against carrying out her threat.

Undaunted and still furious at her husband, Constance began to talk to federal authorities, giving them valuable information. At that time the government was investigating Ormento and half a dozen other major Mafia figures for narcotics violations. Constance warned the officials that the Mafia was planning to kill their key witness. To prove the accuracy of her information she told them the address of the house in New Jersey where the witness was being held—a secret known only to a few government agents.

The government saved the witness's life and ultimately won its case against the high-powered Mafiosi, who were convicted and received heavy sentences. But before they could make a case against Philip Rastelli, the irrepressible Constance was shot to death, a victim of Mafia vengeance.

The life of a Mafia girl friend is even less enviable than that of a Mafia wife. For one thing, the girl friends seem much more likely to come to a bloody end along with their inamoratos. Anthony Colombo, for example, the father of the Joseph Colombo who founded the Italian-American Civil Rights League, was found strangled in an automobile in 1938. With him was the body of a woman friend, Christine Oliveri, who had also been garroted.

One Mafia girl friend showed such admirable presence of mind in a difficult situation that it eventually won her a highly placed underworld husband. The girl was spending a weekend in Florida with her gangster boy friend, when he suddenly died of a heart attack. Before doing anything else, according to police, she called two Mafia friends to come over and search his still-warm body for any evidence that might incriminate fellow family members. Only then did she call an ambulance. This display of cool thinking under stress so impressed a major New York gambling figure that she is today the gambler's wife.

The vast majority of Mafia girl friends, however, soon discover the sad truth: although a Mafioso may be a very generous lover, he will almost never divorce his wife for his girl friend. This, of course, is a universal tendency of the married male, but the Mafioso, especially, respects the old double standard that holds that there are good women (one's wife and mother) and bad women (who are fun to sleep with) and each must be carefully kept in a separate niche.

The old-time Mafiosi—the Mustache Petes, who were born in Sicily and brought the Cosa Nostra to the United States—had very strict sexual codes and frowned on members having mistresses at all. Mustache Petes, Giuseppe Masseria among them, even blocked the entry of Al Capone into the Mafia for a good many years because they disapproved of the fact that he made money from prostitution.

The modern Mafia leader, however, finds a good-looking mistress—preferably several—as important an accessory as a diamond pinky ring or a Miami Beach suntan. One such interesting revelation emerged when the FBI, under court order, released conversations picked up by a bug in the office of Sam "The Plumber" DeCavalcante, the boss of a small New Jersey Mafia family, and a married man. In addition to more significant facts about the life of a Mafia boss, the transcript revealed that Sam was carrying on an affair with his secretary, Harriet Gold, who was also the sister of Larry Wolfson, Sam's partner in the plumbing business. Not only was Sam cheating on his wife with Harriet, he was also cheating on Harriet with a number of other women. He frequently told each of them, including his wife, how much he loved her. He also got a kick out of talking to Harriet's husband on one telephone line while whispering endearments to her on another.

As the affair progressed, Harriet complained to Sam that she was uncomfortable when she and her husband and Sam and his wife were together, that Sam did not call her as often as he promised, that she did not get along with her husband any longer, and that she was no longer sleeping with him. Sam, meanwhile, continued to take discreet weekend trips with other women and emphasized to Harriet, when necessary, his respect for his wife, Mary, and their children.

The tapes also revealed Sam in his "godfather" role. He arranged for his Mafia family to pay for the wedding of his underboss's daughter. He also attempted to help sort out the troubled marriage of one Frank Perrone, who had left his wife. Both were children of alleged members of his Mafia family. Sam agreed, in a conversation with a friend, that both Frank Perrone and his father were rotten because they had both assured Sam that the marriage would be a success. The friend suggested that Sam get together with a relative of the Perrones' who might persuade Frank to do the right thing by his wife. This interest by a Mafia boss in an underling's private life and the lives of his sons and daughters is not unusual. Even the marriages of a soldier's children are sometimes subject to veto by the soldier's *capo*.

Sam also took a godfatherly interest in close

friends who were not Mafia members, such as his partner Larry Wolfson. Larry told Sam that he was trying to turn a young female relative of his into a lady, and he asked for Sam's advice. Should he bring the girl to New York from California, where she was living? Sam replied that he had already had the girl investigated and that she was no good: she was out every night with a different man. "She steals, she drinks, and she doesn't care who she goes out with," said Sam. He added that he loved Larry like a son, "so take my advice and leave her in California." Sam's motivation for having Larry's relative investigated was not solely altruistic. Any unstable person, such as a woman who drinks and runs around with men, can become a potential chink in a Mafia family's armor.

The Mafia woman most deserving of pity is the Mafia daughter. She did not choose her way of life, but she has difficulty escaping it. Her love life and her virtue become matters of great interest to everyone in her father's Mafia family. Until recently her marriage was likely to be arranged for political reasons to bolster the strength of the Mafia family, and she might not have known the groom who had been selected for her.

Today, however, according to law enforcement authorities, more and more Mafia daughters are meeting and marrying men outside the Mafia. One reason is the increased tendency of all young people to travel. Another is the fact that Mafia daughters are, as a rule, sent away to college. "Their fathers tend to use the college level more as a finishing school than as a first step to a career," said one federal agent. But some daughters will later go into a serious career, such as buyer for a large department store, often with a little behind-the-scenes boost from Daddy.

There are other advantages to being a Mafia daughter. Joseph Profaci, the late Brooklyn Mafia boss also known as the Olive Oil King, named his olive oil for his daughter Carmela. A Boston Mafioso set aside $10,000 annually for his daughter and gave her the whole bundle when she turned twenty-one. And many Mafia leaders are particularly solicitous of their daughters' virtue. For example, when Carmine Lombardozzi, a married Mafioso, started a relationship with the daughter of a reputed Mafia soldier, the girl's irate father complained to the leadership. The leaders in turn issued an ultimatum to Lombardozzi: either marry the girl or leave her alone. After thinking it over, Lombardozzi decided to divorce his wife of nearly thirty years and go through with the wedding. His ex-wife proved remarkably amenable and the pair remained on good terms.

Some daughters inherit the toughness of their fathers along with a dangerous independence of spirit. One such girl, the daughter of a Florida-based underworld racketeer and financial genius, shook the entire underworld with her doings several years ago. Used to having her way, she threw over her Mafia boy friend for a passionate affair with a singer well known in the Miami area. The rejected Mafioso did not take kindly to the slight.

Before long, the door of the singer's plush hotel room was found peppered with bullet holes. Although no one was hurt, this made the girl so angry that she did the one thing the underworld cannot accept—she went to the police. Ultimately the rejected suitor was severely reprimanded and the girl was left in peace with her singer, but not before her father had received a harsh tongue-lashing from his fellow racketeers. Only his very high position in the hierarchy prevented bloodshed.

Few daughters of Mafiosi are as assertive as the Miami girl. Most of them accept the rules that go with the life into which they were born. Until recently, when marriage outside the Mafia became acceptable, those rules called for dutiful Mafia daughters to become dutiful Mafia wives.

Some Mafia daughters were coaxed into marrying sons of Mafiosi who belonged to groups with which their fathers wanted to cement business ties. Others fell in love and married within the groups to which their fathers, brothers, uncles, and cousins belonged. All this resulted in many Mafia groups becoming closely inbred. In one case, for example, two daughters of a Mafioso married two brothers who were part of the same Mafia group that their father belonged to. The brothers were distant cousins of the girls. Twenty-five years later a son of one of the couples and a daughter of the second fell in love and married. They had five children, three of whom were born mentally retarded. "There are many instances of defective children in Mafia families because of the inbreeding through the years," says a federal agent. "I'm sure that is one reason why Mafiosi now allow their children to marry outside the Mafia."

Those women who have married within the Mafia, however, are expected to possess two qualities above all others—loyalty and silence. But even a good Mafia wife can come to grief if she makes the mistake of knowing too much about her husband's rackets. "Trigger Mike" Coppola, an important figure in the New York numbers racket, had a dark-eyed wife named Doris, whom he loved. She was present on the day that Mike and a friend discussed a certain Republican district captain in Mike's home. The next day the district captain was beaten, and six days later he died.

During the investigation of the murder, Mrs. Coppola vanished. A search for her as a possible witness in the case was launched and she eventually surrendered. On the basis of her testimony before a grand jury, she was charged with perjury. Now she was in a difficult position: if she told the truth, her husband would go to jail; if she refused to talk, she would go to jail. To make matters worse, Doris was pregnant. While she was still under indictment, a daughter was born, and the next day Mrs. Coppola died, thus solving everyone's problems. Her husband, contrary to his religion, had the body cremated.

Everyone assumed that Doris had died of complications of childbirth, but many years later, Trigger Mike's second wife claimed she found papers in a safe that indicated that Mike had had his beloved wife killed. According to acquaintances, he never quite got over her death.

Any man who puts his love for his wife before his sense of "justice" loses face with his fellow gangsters. This is what happened to Vito Genovese, one of the most powerful Mafia figures in the United States before his death in Atlanta Penitentiary in 1970.

In December of 1952 Genovese's wife, Anna, left their home in New Jersey and sued for divorce on the grounds that his cruelty "endangered her health and made her life extremely wretched." During the divorce proceedings she portrayed her husband as a vicious mob leader with a vast income. She talked about the location of safe-deposit boxes full of cash in the United States and in Europe. She discussed his involvement in gambling, nightclubs, loan-sharking, and labor-union kickbacks. The Mafia could hardly believe that she was being allowed to give such testimony, but Genovese, who was still in love with her, did not have the courage to kill her.

"The word was all around, why didn't he hit [kill] her," Joseph Valachi later recalled. "But he must have really cared for her . . . I remember when we—Vito and me—were in Atlanta [Penitentiary] together later on, he would sometimes talk about her, and I would see the tears rolling down his cheeks. I couldn't believe it."

But Genovese had no compassion for the man he had assigned to keep an eye on Anna, Steve Franse. Valachi said Genovese had had him killed for not performing this duty adequately.

Franse was not the only man connected with Anna to meet a violent death. Her first husband, Gerard Vernotico, was murdered twelve days before Anna married Genovese in a civil ceremony. Valachi said that Genovese had ordered Vernotico killed so that the beautiful Anna would be free to marry him.

Genovese's passion for Anna weakened him in the eyes of the mob because few Mafia husbands are so soft-hearted toward their wives. Indeed some of them carry home with them the violence and sadism that make them so feared in the underworld, as Ann Drahmann, Trigger Mike Coppola's second wife, discovered.

Ann was born to Italian parents in 1921 in Cincinnati. She grew into a dark-eyed, dark-haired beauty and at the age of sixteen found herself pregnant and married to a young sailor. As soon as a daughter was born, the marriage was over. Ann became a waitress in a mob-owned restaurant-bar-casino in Covington, Kentucky. She caught the eye of the casino manager, Charles Drahmann, a small time gangster, and eventually they were married.

When Ann was thirty-one, Drahmann and his boss were killed in the crash of a private plane, and Ann was left a widow without much money. She opened a dress shop and frequently gave parties at which local gangsters were guests.

In 1955 Ann was invited to attend the Marciano-Moore fight in New York in the company of three Newport, Kentucky, gangsters and their wives. Although they did not mention it to her, the real purpose of the trip was to introduce Ann to Trigger Mike Coppola, the fat, swarthy, five-foot-five boss of the numbers racket in East Harlem and an overlord of the Eastern Syndicate. His first wife, Doris, had met an untimely death, as we have seen, and Mike was looking for a replacement. His gangster friends had picked Ann as a likely candidate after making sure that she was not promiscuous or otherwise unsuited to be the wife of such an important man.

Trigger Mike was enchanted with Ann. After a short courtship, during which he bombarded her with jewels, candy, and flowers, they were married on December 28, 1955, in Lawrenceburg, Indiana. When it was all over Mike paid for the reception with a $1,000 bill.

Because New York had become a bit too hot for him, Mike had moved to a luxurious house in Miami Beach, and it was there that he installed his new bride. Unfortunately, Ann was too nosy for her own good and unearthed a number of "plants"—secret hiding places behind walls and sliding bookcases—where her husband secreted vast amounts of cash, as most important mob figures do. Mike rewarded her for her discoveries with a vicious beating, the first of many. Soon she discovered that he had a strong sadistic streak that included rather bizarre practices.

When Ann became pregnant, her husband insisted on calling in an underworld doctor, who performed an abortion on her while she lay on the kitchen table and Trigger Mike helped. She quickly realized that this was her husband's idea of a really good time. He assisted at four abortions in all until, during the fifth pregnancy, she managed to fake a miscarriage, which was then treated at a hospital.

In spite of the beatings and abortions, Ann felt that her life as the wife of an important Mafia figure had its compensations. They traveled annually to the Kentucky Derby and on occasion to Las Vegas on gambling junkets. Whenever Ann would say "the girls and I want to do a little gambling," Mike would call friends in pre-Castro Havana to get them the best hotel suites and unlimited credit. Mike, eager to show off his status, gave her jewels, furs, and cars. He also handed her large sums of money for her own use, which she carefully stashed away after noting down the amount in a little black book. In four years her hoard of cash amounted to $277,100.

By this time Ann had come to feel that life with Trigger Mike was no longer tolerable. After her daughter from a previous marriage graduated from private school at the age of eighteen, she had come to live with them, and Ann felt that Mike was showing an unhealthy interest in the girl. During one of their violent fights Mike revealed to Ann that he had been providing her daughter with drugs.

In 1960, after one last bloody fight, Ann and her daughter moved out. Prudently Ann had sneaked her cash and jewels out of the house before she left. Mike filed for divorce, charging that her "vile and abusive language" would make delinquents of his children by his previous marriage. She filed a cross-claim charging him with extreme cruelty. Their final divorce decree was signed on March 25. He agreed to pay her $25,000 in cash and another $25,000 under the table.

At about this time, an agent of the Internal Revenue Service approached Ann and asked if she would help with an audit of her husband's tax returns by giving information on his income and expenditures. For the sake of vengeance, she agreed. Trigger Mike, who had given her $277,100 in four years, had reported his income to the IRS as $15,000 in 1957 and $31,087 in 1958. He claimed that these sums had been earned at the racetrack.

The jewelry that Ann had carried off with her was estimated by the IRS to be worth $40,000. Every day she gave detailed information to the IRS agents even though, on one occasion, she was kidnapped from her hotel, beaten up, and left on a beach in a state of shock. United States Attorney General Robert Kennedy then ordered that she be guarded twenty-four hours a day at an Air Force base near the Florida Keys.

Ann poured out every detail of her life with Trigger Mike as the IRS prepared its case against him. She estimated Mike's income from the rackets to be at least $1 million a year. In 1961 he was indicted on four counts of income tax evasion. But the trial, at which Ann would testify, was months away, and she wanted to travel to Europe with her daughter and enjoy a little of her freedom and money.

The IRS strongly advised against the trip because the FBI had learned from informants in the underworld that Ann had been marked for death in Europe and would disappear. But Ann stubbornly refused to cancel her plans and IRS men in Europe were alerted to keep an eye on her. At a casino in France Ann and her daughter were picked up by two "charming men" who followed them to Geneva before Ann decided they might be murderers. She evaded them and continued on to Italy, where Trigger Mike's attorney found her and tried to convince her not to return to the United States.

In November of 1961 Ann was flown back to New York and kept in hiding before appearing at the trial in Miami. Then, at the last minute before the trial, two jurors unexpectedly admitted that they had read newspaper stories alleging that Mike was a gangster, and a third juror said that he had watched a TV news account of the impending trial. A mistrial was declared, and the case was rescheduled for three months later. Ann had a tantrum and boarded a plane for Miami, threatening to shoot her ex-husband. On the flight an IRS agent managed to calm her down and coax her into giving up her pistol.

When the trial finally opened, Mike unexpectedly pleaded guilty before Ann could testify. It was generally believed that the mob had decided that this was the course he must take in order to prevent damaging secrets about his rackets from being aired in court. He was condemned to serve a year and a day on each of four counts, the sentences to run concurrently, and he was ordered to pay a $40,000 fine. He was also placed on four years probation when his sentence expired.

Mike served his time in the federal prison near Atlanta, where Mafiosi like Vito Genovese and Joe Valachi were among his fellow prisoners. After his release, most of his underworld friends made it clear that they regarded him as a fool, both for allowing his wife to learn his secrets and for being unable to stop her from talking. In October of 1966 Trigger Mike died of undisclosed causes in an expensive Boston hospital room.

After Mike's trial Ann returned to Rome, where six months later she committed suicide by washing down an overdose of Nembutal with a lot of scotch. She had been marked by the mob as a stoolie and an outcast, and she was to have been killed.

Ann left a number of letters, including one to the Internal Revenue Service representative at the American Embassy in Paris. In it she addressed, among others, Robert Kennedy and her daughter, Joan. Her last words in the letter were for her ex-husband, Trigger Mike: "Mike Coppola, someday, somehow, a person or God or the Law shall catch up with you, you yellow-bellied bastard. You are the lowest and biggest coward I have had the misfortune to meet."

With her pen still clutched in her hand, she was found dead on her bed in an ultrafashionable Roman hotel. On the wall above the bed she had written: "I have always suffered. I am going to kill myself. Forget me."

7

BIAS IN THE MAFIA

THE MAFIA is not an equal opportunity employer.

That is probably the least of the worries caused by one of America's biggest, most profitable businesses to federal, state, and local authorities. But it certainly rankles the black hood who wants to get ahead.

"A black man's got a better chance of being elected mayor of Selma, Alabama, than of making it into the big money with the mob," grumbles one Brooklyn black. Formerly a numbers runner for a bank operated by a Mafioso, he quit when he could not get a promotion to controller and now is in business for himself as a pimp. (Controllers oversee groups of runners for the "bank," or management center, of a numbers operation.)

The disgruntled Brooklynite is only one of many blacks who have discovered a fundamental fact about the Mafia's personnel policies—no door is more firmly locked to blacks than the one that leads to the halls of power in organized crime. This is ironic considering that the black—especially the poor black—is the most frequent victim of the lords of crime. As will be detailed in Chapter 8, the ghettos contribute a big share of the organized underworld's estimated annual take of $2 billion from the numbers racket and $500 million from narcotics, according to law enforcement officials. These authorities, however, see few black necks in the white collars of the men who run these rackets.

There is little an affronted black gangster can do about the situation. He can hardly go to his local human rights commission charging job bias, and it is considered dangerous to complain too loudly to one's boss, who might find it a symptom of excessive ambition. Therapy can be fatal, occasionally involving the gun, the knife, or the cement overshoe.

Nevertheless, a group of black gangsters in New York threw caution to the winds in 1968 and kidnapped several prominent Mafiosi. They did not harm them, but they pointed out to them in strong terms that they wanted some share of the profits from ghetto rackets. The Mafiosi, according to police, refused to cut them in on rackets already established but agreed to let them start a small number of new operations on their own. As a result there are now a few black numbers banks in New York and a small number of black narcotics wholesalers.

For the most part, however, blacks in the employ of the Mafia and the numerous affiliates and subsidiaries that make up organized crime remain blue-collar workers. They function primarily in such risky but still menial jobs as narcotics peddlers or numbers runners. At the present time police know of few blacks who are in a position to draw a substantial share of organized crime profits.

The kingpins of the underworld, not a notably chatty group, offer no explanation for this apparent policy of racial discrimination. However, a prosperous Boston loan shark, whose work brings him in close contact with Mafiosi, says: "Most of the big boys don't want them in responsible positions. You need people you can be sure about in this business. You feel better with your own kind, you know what I mean?"

Federal law enforcement officials agree that Jewish, Irish, and Italian mobsters do tend to hire and promote from within their own ethnic groups. Still, there is a lot more tolerance and accommodation among white ethnic groups than those movie battles between Al Capone and Bugs Moran would indicate. Actually, racketeers from various groups of white gangsters have been sharing tasks and dividing profits under the umbrella of the organized crime syndicate for many years. Federal agents, for example, demonstrate the rich diversity of ethnic backgrounds in the underworld by pointing to the leading figures in organized crime in Chicago—Tony Accardo, Gus Alex, Murray Humphreys, Paul Rica, Ralph Pierce, Leonard Patrick, Elias Argyropoulos, Lester Kruse.

In some cases, the ethnic barriers within separate units of organized crime seem to be lowering a bit, too. As will be shown in Chapter 9, the Mafia, which once handled the bulk of the heroin traffic in the United States, turned over certain high-risk parts of the business to Cuban and South American gangsters early in the 1960's. However, few such "employment opportunities" have been given to blacks in the underworld.

The only black ever to achieve any prominence in the ranks of organized crime was Ellsworth "Bumpy" Johnson, who died in 1968. He had served three long terms for peddling narcotics and was under a federal indictment on a similar charge when he died at sixty-two of a heart attack. While in prison, Johnson studied history and philosophy and became an expert chess player.

He also began to write poetry, and three of his poems were published in *Freedomways,* "a quarterly review of the Negro freedom movement."

In New York's Harlem, where he was a famous figure for forty years, Johnson spent money lavishly and won the envy and admiration of many blacks. In fact, white mobsters used him to exploit other blacks. A Harlem newsman described him accurately at his well-attended funeral as a "contract man . . . [who] handled the disciplinary action within the rackets families. When a man was rebelling in the black area against white control, enforcement contracts went through Bumpy."

Bumpy Johnson took the only safe road open for a black gangster—exploitation of fellow blacks —and he managed to die of natural causes. Those who have tried to make money in the rackets by competing against white gangsters have not been so lucky. Cases in point are the two ambitious blacks who tried to build names for themselves in the Cincinnati rackets. The first was Steve "Bull" Payne, who late in the forties organized a big numbers network in the city. On March 23, 1948, his well-ventilated corpse was found in a ditch. Within a year, his network was being run by Frank Andrews (born Andriola), a local Mafia chief then operating out of Newport, Kentucky.

Seven years later another black, Melvin Clark, also began to gain prominence in the Cincinnati rackets. On July 18, 1955, he, too, was found shot to death. Frank Andrews was charged with the murder but was acquitted. (He was later convicted on charges stemming from his gambling operations and sent to federal prison.)

These harsh measures are usually taken only in extreme cases of excessive ambition. More often, the black who seems to be getting big ideas suffers a gentler fate, perhaps arrest by police who are on the syndicate payroll. This serves to get him out of the way for a time with no messy complications, but it does little to help the police image in black neighborhoods.

"In the ghettos, contempt for the police is partly rooted in the knowledge that some of them are serving the white racketeers who are bleeding the community," contends Lincoln Lynch, Associate National Director of the Congress of Racial Equality.

A few years ago blacks in Harlem tried to turn the tables on the white gangsters by giving information about them to police and politicians. Former Harlem Congressman Adam Clayton Powell even read on the floor of the House the names of whites prominent in ghetto rackets. Nothing came of this effort.

Blacks probably had more opportunity in the rackets fifty years ago than they do today. Until late in the 1920's they ran big numbers networks. White mobsters, busy raking in profits from bootlegging, viewed numbers profits as measly and referred to the numbers contemptuously as "nigger pool."

But as the future of bootlegging darkened, it dawned on organized crime that the numbers could be profitable indeed. The first to see the potential in numbers was New York mobster Dutch Schultz, who dispatched his legions into Harlem early in the 1930's to take over. The late Malcolm X, once a numbers runner there, recalled what happened in his autobiography. "I heard many stories . . . how they [the Schultz mob] persuaded people with lead pipes, wet cement, baseball bats, brass knuckles, fists, feet and blackjacks," he wrote.

Similar campaigns of persuasion soon were under way in other urban ghettos, and before long the numbers racket passed into the control of white gangsters, where it remains today. "The mobs exploit the ghettos the way some companies exploited banana republics in the old days. They squeeze millions out of them and leave pennies behind," says Hank Messick, author of *The Silent Syndicate* and other books on organized crime.

The significance of racial prejudice in the underworld may go beyond the money that white gangsters have taken from the black ghettos. Daniel Bell, the noted sociologist, has suggested that crime may have served as an instrument of upward mobility for minority groups in American society. According to his theory, there has been "ethnic succession" in crime in the United States. It is his belief that the Irish, Jews, and Italians each produced a strong criminal element after arriving here in great numbers and that this element used its influence to secure political power for its own ethnic group. Bell points out, for example, that there were practically no Italian judges in New York until Frank Costello, the reputed Mafioso, temporarily gained a hold on Democratic politics in the city.

If Bell's theory is correct (and many doubt it), the bias that has kept black gangsters from becoming powerful in organized crime may have denied all blacks a proper share of political power in America.

Despite the underworld establishment's tendency to shun blacks except as targets for exploitation, more benevolent attitudes occasionally crop up. The notorious brothers Larry and Albert Gallo of Brooklyn, for example, helped cool a 1965 racial explosion between Italian-Americans and blacks in East New York at the request of the city's Youth Board.

Another brother, Joseph "Crazy Joe" Gallo, even played a role in furthering desegregation in public accommodations—at Attica Prison, where he was sent in 1961 following a conviction for extortion. According to one insider, he earned the wrath of fellow white inmates when he insisted that white barbers cut blacks' hair.

But there apparently are not enough white gangsters like the Gallos to make a difference. Most blacks could be forgiven a bitter chuckle at the fictional Buonaparte Ignace Gallia, called Mr. Big, a hulking Negro who ran an immense criminal network from his Harlem headquarters in Ian Fleming's novel *Live and Let Die*. In the real underworld all the Mr. Bigs are white.

8

ORGANIZED CRIME IN THE GHETTO

WHEN SEVERAL HUNDRED Puerto Rican youths ran through New York's East Harlem on the night of June 14, 1970, smashing store windows and setting rubbish fires after a rally to protest the arrest of a Young Lords leader, almost every store between 105th and 116th streets suffered some damage.

One of the few to survive with hardly a scratch was the East Harlem Pet Shop, on Second Avenue and 112th Street. The pet shop was owned by Samuel "Big Sam" Cavalieri, who has been named by law enforcement officials as a leading gambler and loan shark in East Harlem and a key figure in the Mafia family of the late Thomas Luchese. Even youths on the rampage know better than to mess with Big Sam.

Organized crime in the slums is not the monopoly of the Mafia however; is also includes Jewish, Puerto Rican, Cuban, and black gangsters. It is impossible to determine exactly how much money organized crime squeezes out of the slums. But the New York State Joint Legislative Committee on Crime estimated that in 1968 alone, the revenues from illicit narcotics and gambling in New York City's three main slum areas—Central Harlem, the South Bronx, and the Bedford-Stuyvesant section of Brooklyn—was $343 million. That represents $70 million more than the state spent on welfare in the same areas.

"The flow of money from the ghetto to organized crime is so great that there can be little meaningful economic improvement in New York City's ghettos until it is stopped," says state Senator John Hughes of Syracuse, chairman of the Crime Committee.

All slum residents are victimized. Drug pushers reach the young and the weak in the streets; loan sharks reach laborers and office workers at their jobs; numbers runners reach housewives, shopkeepers, salesgirls, and welfare recipients in their homes and neighborhoods.

The most lucrative slum operation for organ-

ntroller sheets. Raymond Marquez was
sentially because the FBI found a sin-
int on a master sheet in the New Jer-
his lieutenant, Radames Mas.

erlings who do handle incriminating
e sometimes arrested when they are
d by payoffs to police, but the bosses
ouble finding others to replace them.
us circle," said Seymour Rotker, chief
ts division in the office of Bronx Dis-
ey Burton R. Roberts. "The only way
g to get those at the top is through
on of wire taps."

has five lieutenants in addition to
as convicted with him. Four are former
One was dismissed from the New
Department after eight years on the
etired when disabled by an accident,
is receiving a pension after being a
or twenty years. Law enforcement of-
nat numbers operators like to employ
emen because of their contacts.

on uncovered in the investigation of
ez empire shows that approximately
onth, or 7.5 per cent of the profit, was
graft. The total volume of the Mar-
ion is believed to be $25 million a year.
t margin that is said to be 15 per cent,
ez operation nets approximately $3.7
ar.

ized crime is the numbers racket. The policy game, as it is sometimes called, is played by 75 per cent of all adult and late-teen-aged slum residents in New York. Each of them spends an average of $3 to $5 a week on it, according to the Hughes committee. The stakes may not seem high, but they mount up when several members of a family play every day. In fact, based on current population figures for Harlem, South Bronx, and Bedford-Stuyvesant, government officials estimate that more than $150 million is spent on the numbers in the three areas every year, almost all of it in games run by organized crime.

Profits from the numbers also finance police corruption and reinforce other, more destructive rackets. "One of my clerks borrowed money from loan sharks to do some heavy betting on the numbers and wound up pushing dope to pay off the loan sharks," said a fruit-store operator in Central Harlem. Malcolm X writes in his autobiography of gambling away all the tips he earned as a waiter—"as high as $15 and $20 a day"—on the numbers.

Slum residents who play the numbers are pursuing what James Baldwin has called "the American dream in blackface"—the chance of making a "hit," selecting the winning three-digit number for the day and winning $600 on a $1 bet.

The behind-the-scenes workings of one numbers operation, that of Raymond Marquez, who is known as Spanish Raymond, shows how profitable and efficient the racket is. The Marquez network is ranked by law enforcement officials as the fifth largest in New York City. It is testament to Marquez's organizational skill that his operation continues even though Marquez himself has been in jail since January, 1970.

Marquez operated freely until the Federal Bureau of Investigation moved against him in 1969. He was arrested and tried with his chief lieutenant, Radames Mas, on charges of violating federal gambling laws. Both were convicted; while out on appeal, Marquez was re-arrested on similar charges by the FBI and remanded to jail.

Court records, information from law enforcement officials, and interviews with slum residents provide a clear picture of the Marquez operation. His five banks, which are centered in Harlem, employ a total of about four hundred runners, who fan out in the neighborhoods collecting bets from customers. In addition, Marquez has a number of "spots," usually stores, where clients can place bets. Among the spots Marquez has used, according to the law enforcement officials, is the Caribe Florist Shop, which is owned by two of his brothers, Fernando and Robert.

Next in line are twenty-seven controllers, usually store owners, who record the bets brought in by each runner and send the information to the bank, or "office," via a pickup man. Marquez's

pickup people are ir
old people or young gi
salary, usually about $

The controllers get
runners collect. From
them to handle such "
fees if their runners
reasons his controllers
they have collected wit
they settle up periodica
tative, who keeps their ta

The FBI raided one
a betting volume that so
a day. Based in an ap
Florist Shop, the bank
system connected to the
so solidly encased in me
not break it down. Inste
through a wall to get in.

The New York police
Marquez bank, operated
uncle, Angelica and San
ment in the Bronx sectic
pleaded guilty to posse
Despite the raids, all f
operation again.

Numbers operations
and numbers operators
bars—because only und
evidence that stands u

slips and c
convicted
gle finger
sey home o

The u
evidence
not prote
have no
"It's a vi
of the ra
trict Atto
you're g
the utili

Marqu
Mas, wh
policeme
York Po
force, or
and a t
policema
ficials sa
former p

Inform
the Mar
$25,000 a
set aside
quez ope
With a p
the Mar
million a

Most of the money does not stay in Harlem. Although the majority of the runners and some of the controllers are black residents of Harlem, those at the top are not. Marquez himself has a $100,000 home at 40 Keats Lane, Great Neck, Long Island. He also has substantial real-estate holdings both here and abroad, as well as a thick portfolio of securities, according to records found during the investigation of his empire.

Marquez's success in the numbers racket is proof that you do not have to be in the Mafia to do well in organized crime. He was born to Puerto Rican parents in New York forty years ago. Members of his family established close ties to Mafia leaders, however, which have helped him through the years.

According to government sources, his father was a numbers operator for the late Mafia boss Vito Genovese; his brother Lionel was convicted on a narcotics charge in the same case that finally sent Genovese to prison; and Raymond himself showed such talent that Anthony "Fat Tony" Salerno, the big boss of the Mafia rackets in Harlem, gave him his own bank at an early age. Marquez reportedly still pays 5 per cent of his profits to Salerno, partly in gratitude and partly because anybody who operates in Harlem has to pay Fat Tony something.

Salerno, who now lives in Florida but frequently commutes to New York, is absentee boss of a $50-

million-a-year numbers operation—the biggest in Harlem. His empire reportedly is divided among three lieutenants, Louis "The Gimp" Avitabile, Salvatore Apuzzo, and Louis Vigilante.

The East Harlem operation of Big Sam Cavalieri, whose pet shop was left undamaged in the June, 1970, riot, is one of several that belong to members of the Thomas Luchese family. But in Harlem the Luchese empire is overshadowed by that of Salerno, who is a key figure in the Genovese family.

Law enforcement officials also identify several other underworld figures who command lucrative rackets in New York's ghettos. In the South Bronx the major figures in the numbers racket are the Schlitten brothers, Samuel and Moishe, better known as Sam and Moe, whose banks do an annual betting volume of more than $30 million. The Schlittens operate in association with several members of the Genovese and Luchese Mafia families, who get a percentage of the profit. The Mafia partners, law enforcement officials say, keep a close watch on Sam Schlitten for two reasons: he is a chronic gambler who has been known to lose $50,000 of the operation's money in one night at dice and cards, and he likes to take frequent vacations in Florida, leaving his less competent brother in charge.

The Mafiosi tolerate his excesses, however, because Sam Schlitten has a reputation for running a numbers network better than any other man in New York. His police record goes back to 1928, when he was jailed for robbery. In 1931 he was questioned—and then released—about the brief kidnapping of Lita Grey, the former wife of comedian Charlie Chaplin. Neither he nor Moishe has served time for gambling violations.

The dominant figure in Bedford-Stuyvesant is Paul Vario, one of the Luchese family, according to government sources. His empire is believed to be almost as profitable as that of the Schlitten brothers. Vario lives in Island Park, Long Island.

The biggest operator in Brooklyn, indeed in all New York, is James Napoli, known as Jimmy Nap, whose enterprises are said to gross about $70 million a year. His network is centered in the Williamsburg-Greenpoint section. It touches the fringes of the slum but focuses on middle-class neighborhoods.

Jimmy Nap is an independent sort who has turned down many invitations from friends in the Mafia to join the organization. His rackets include gambling on sports as well as the numbers. He lives in a $150,000 Manhattan townhouse.

Blacks never used to rise higher than controller in the numbers hierarchy partly because of race prejudice among white gangsters and partly because slum residents feared that their fellow blacks would not be able to pay off heavy winnings without the resources of established banks.

But now, law enforcement officials say, some blacks are gaining a toehold in the slums. Thomas Greene, whose numbers network is in Central Harlem, has a substantial bank in operation. A second black bank in Harlem is operated by Fritz Devenish and Clarence Hales, who are known as Fritz and Crappy.

In Bedford-Stuyvesant at least two substantial black banks are in operation, one headed by Peter Mooney and the second by Edward "Brother" Gibbs. Mooney's operation is connected to Vario's, but Gibbs is more or less on his own.

Narcotics, too, have been traditionally the monopoly of established gangsters, particularly the Mafia. But in recent years Mafiosi have been turning over some of the high-risk aspects of the narcotics trade to other groups. Still, as will be demonstrated in the next chapter, Mafiosi continue to handle the overseas arrangements and provide the capital for bulk purchases. In return they get a percentage of the impressive profits.

The New York State Joint Legislative Committee on Crime estimates that the gross revenue from the narcotics traffic in New York's three major slum areas "ranges from a minimum of $122 million annually to $238 million."

In addition to the rake-off it gets for underwriting the drug traffic, the Mafia earns millions more as an indirect result of narcotics. It operates several networks of "fences," who buy the goods stolen by addicts to support their habit. A study of three thousand addicts by the State Narcotic Addiction Control Commission revealed that the average addict needs about $30 a day for drugs. To get it, he has to steal an average of more than $35,000 worth of property a year.

The addicts try to sell the goods themselves, and they also sell to the fences, who pay 20 per cent of the value of the goods. Organized crime networks then sell the goods to clients throughout the country at two to three times what they paid, which is still low enough for retailers to make a nice profit. Again, it is the slums that suffer most. About 75 per cent of the heroin addicts in New York are black or Puerto Rican, and they first rob the homes and stores in their own neighborhoods, the Hughes committee says.

Loan-sharking is a third way in which organized crime squeezes money out of the slums. Interest rates range as high as 20 per cent a week. Loan sharks like to catch slum residents at their jobs, make them small loans, and then start squeezing. For example, Franklin Roberts (not his real name), a Harlem resident who works in the garment district, borrowed $10 early last year at the usual 20 per cent interest from a loan shark in his shop. He promised to repay the loan the next payday, according to the story he told government officials. When the day came, he was still hard up for cash and was relieved to see that the loan shark was not around. But three days later the loan shark appeared and asked for his money.

"You should have caught me payday," Roberts recalled telling the loan shark. "I'm really low now."

"All right," said the loan shark, "give me a couple of bucks now, and I'll let you go another week." When the week was up, the same routine took place, and for many weeks afterward Roberts found that paying the $2 was much easier than paying the $10 he owed. By the time he finally repaid the $10 principal, he had given the loan shark $84 in interest.

It was a typical transaction, which also reveals that the loan shark, contrary to popular impression, does not rush to break a client's arms and legs if the payments are a little late. Loan sharks are as much con men as muscle men, and they prefer to milk slum residents as long as they can. Only when the interest payments stop will they turn to more forceful methods.

Loan sharks haunt shops, docks, construction sites, and offices as well as the slums. Most numbers operators, for example, use loan-sharking as a way of investing their profits from gambling. Law enforcement officials believe that Salerno, Vario, and the Schlitten brothers are heavily involved in loan-sharking.

Slum residents are at the mercy of loan sharks

because many blacks and Puerto Ricans are frequently refused loans by legitimate sources. Loan sharks have no fear that these customers will betray them because betrayal would mean cutting off their only source of money until payday or the arrival of the next welfare check.

"If it was not for the existence of organized crime, many of the social conditions that exist in our community would be unable to exist," Congressman Charles B. Rangel of Harlem told a state investigating committee last year.

The Reverend Dr. Martin Luther King put it more strongly. "Organized crime," he said, "is the nightmare of the slum family."

9

ORGANIZED CRIME AND NARCOTICS

FEBRUARY 24–25, 1969. In a warehouse on a pier in Brooklyn, United States Customs agents and police officers spend the night examining with a special x-ray machine a shipment of 702 cases of canned sardines from Spain. They find that two of the cases make an unusual pattern on the x-ray screen. When one of these cases is opened, all the sardine cans in it are found to contain 98 per cent pure heroin. The rest of the shipment is followed to its destination, a private home in Queens, which is put under surveillance. Customs agents eventually arrest two French heroin smugglers who emerge from the house, one of them carrying nearly fifty pounds of heroin packed into a duffel bag. Even while they are in jail awaiting trial, the two Frenchmen arrange for two kilograms of heroin to be shipped to one of their cellmates upon his release from prison. That heroin is part of a shipment smuggled into the United States inside the hollow handles of ski poles.

November, 1965. The possessions of a United States Army warrant officer and his family are shipped from France to Fort Benning, Georgia. Among them is a freezer, its walls stuffed with 190 plastic bags that contain more than 200 pounds of heroin valued at $2.8 million. The Army officer has been paid $10,000 by a friend in France to include the freezer among his belongings. A few weeks after the shipment arrives, two French heroin exporters fly from Paris to New York, and a few days later two Mafiosi named Frank Dioguardi and Anthony Sutera fly from Miami to New York. The Mafiosi and one of the Frenchmen meet in a Manhattan restaurant and make arrangements for the final pickup and transfer of the vast consignment. But before the pickup can be made, the hapless Army officer is arrested by federal agents, who also seize the contents of the freezer, which fill six suitcases. Agents later pick up the Frenchmen and the two Mafiosi.

These cases illustrate the imaginative methods

used to import illegal drugs into the United States, where the contraband ends up in the hands of organized crime. The two main sources of drugs are the Middle East and Southeast Asia.

The fields of bright poppies cultivated in Turkey and a dozen other countries around the world yield bountiful crops of opium, morphine, and heroin. The Turkish farmer who grows poppies for medical use under government license also usually cultivates them secretly for an illegal market. For example, Turkish farmers produce about 180 tons of opium legally every year, and another 100 tons for the black market. Black marketers pay them up to $5 more a pound for their trouble.

The trail of the poppy leads primarily to North America, which is the principal market for illicit heroin. And as heroin, morphine, and opium filter into the country, the insidious harvest swells the coffers of organized crime. No one can know exactly how much money racketeers pocket from the drug traffic, but the estimates are mind-boggling. For instance, there are said to be about 150,000 addicts in the country (nearly half of them in New York City). The average addict, according to the Bureau of Narcotics and Dangerous Drugs, spends $30 a day, or $10,950 a year, to support his habit. (If he is getting that money by stealing, he must steal property worth $36,500 a year.) Thus the revenue from illegal drugs in this country is usually estimated to be close to $2 billion a year. The cost to the taxpayer in stolen goods and funds for the treatment and rehabilitation of addicts is many times higher.

Before World War II the illegal drug market was very limited. Drugs were smuggled into the country by independent criminals and some organized crime figures. With the advent of World War II, the international traffic of heroin completely dried up, and the only illegal narcotics in circulation were those stolen from doctors' offices, drugstores, and hospitals.

But at the end of World War II many American soldiers returned home addicted. Some had encountered narcotics such as cocaine, morphine, heroin, and hashish in Europe and the Middle East; others had become addicted to painkilling drugs during long stays in hospitals. Although the soldier-addicts were not publicized as widely as today's addicted Vietnam veterans, the World War II veterans did expand the market for narcotics. And the growing market attracted more attention from organized crime groups.

Even among the not overly scrupulous racketeers, however, the issue of making money from illegal drugs was an explosive one.* As some mobsters pointed out, it was one thing to profit by liquor, gambling, prostitution, and loan-sharking, but peddling drugs was a different matter. Drugs prey on the young and on the poor who want to escape the misery of their lives, even if only briefly. And drugs often produce a horrible death for the addict who is seeking only euphoria.

But the more hard-nosed and money-minded gangsters, some of whom had dabbled in narcotics before the war, kept pointing to the profits awaiting anyone willing and able to import drugs in a big way. For example, on today's market one kilo (2.2 pounds) of heroin costs about $3,500 in Marseilles. That same kilo, diluted, packaged in small bags, and peddled on the streets of New York will bring $200,000. Not surprisingly, the arithmeticians won out over the moralists.

By the late 1940's and early 1950's, the organized crime families in New York City, mostly Mafia families, were well into the narcotics traffic. There were good reasons why the New York Mafia dominated narcotics. The city was (and still is) the most lucrative market because half of all addicts are located in New York. Furthermore, the European gangsters who processed opium into heroin and smuggled it into Marseilles and other European centers were chiefly Sicilian, and thus were naturally inclined to deal with Mafiosi in the United States.

Initially the Mafia was very pleased with its booming business in illegal drugs, but by the second half of the 1950's the bloom was off the rose. More and more of its members were being arrested, convicted, and sentenced to hefty prison terms. By 1957 Mafia leaders had begun to wonder aloud whether they had made a mistake in entering the narcotics trade in the first place. In fact, one of the main topics on the agenda of the famous summit conference of Mafia leaders at Apalachin, New York, on November 14, 1957, was whether to get out of narcotics completely. Before the meeting could get under way, the Mafiosi were surprised by state police, but the narcotics question assumed new urgency a short time later when Vito Genovese, probably the most powerful Mafia leader of the 1950's, was arrested and convicted on a conspiracy charge involving narcotics. He received a fifteen-year prison term and died behind bars in 1970.

The credit for making the Mafia uneasy about narcotics goes to the federal Bureau of Narcotics, which had developed a number of effective techniques for catching the drug traffickers, including a fine instinct for recognizing potential informants within a drug ring. (The Bureau of Narcotics, which was a part of the Treasury Department for many years, was merged with the Food and Drug Administration's Bureau of Drug Abuse Control in 1968. It was then renamed the Bureau of Narcotics and Dangerous Drugs and transferred to the Department of Justice.)

The decision that the Mafia ultimately made about narcotics was a compromise between the views of those who wanted to get out of the business completely and of those who insisted that the profits were irresistibly high. The Mafia got out of the high-risk retail and smuggling sides of the business, where they were most likely to get caught, but continued to finance heroin purchases and handle some of the low-risk wholesale operations.

The impact of this decision soon became apparent. Early in the 1960's the number of known Mafia figures arrested on drug charges by state and federal agents dropped sharply. The vacuum created when the Mafia pulled out of the high-risk side of the narcotics traffic was quickly filled by Cubans, Latin Americans, Puerto Ricans, and Canadians who were too hungry for the high profits to worry about the dangers.

Some of these groups, especially the Cubans and Latin Americans, quickly formed organizations as strong and efficient as those already in existence, and they have now become full-fledged and honored members of the web of organized crime. One leader of a group of South Americans, Luis Steppenberg, earned the distinction early in 1971 of being held in the highest bail ever set for an individual in the United States—$1.5 million—after he was indicted as the head of one of the biggest narcotics rings in the country. While awaiting sentencing, Steppenberg died in jail on March 11, 1971, of a heart attack, but he amassed quite a fortune while he was alive. In two bank accounts that federal agents discovered, he had $614,000 and $585,000 respectively. On his 1969 tax return Steppenberg had modestly listed an income of $5,800.

In recent years Mafia groups have been easing back into the more dangerous and more lucrative aspects of narcotics. This was reflected by a wave of narcotics arrests in March, 1971, in four major cities including New York. Of the thirty-four persons picked up in the New York area, many of whom were narcotics wholesalers, about half were believed to be associated with Mafia groups.

As of this writing, most federal officials estimate that 90 per cent of the heroin market is evenly divided between the Mafia and other elements of organized crime, notably Cubans and Latin Americans. Lately the number of independents—individuals not connected with criminal organizations—has been growing slightly, but their share of the market is still small.

One of the most colorful of the independent narcotics traffickers was Vivienne Nagelberg, a rotund, middle-aged brunette who has proved to be a veritable Circe when it comes to corrupting people into joining her illegal activities. On June 18, 1970, Vivienne and her husband, Gerson "Jerry" Nagelberg, were both sentenced to fifteen years imprisonment and fined $15,000 for the illegal purchase and receipt of heroin.

Vivienne's downfall began in May, 1967, when narcotics agent Mortimer Benjamin got a tip in his New York office that if he went to Montreal's

Dorval Airport he could intercept two French couriers carrying six kilos of heroin strapped around their waists. He successfully made the arrest, but he was surprised to see that Vivienne was at the airport as well. He recognized her because she had long been suspected of being a major heroin dealer in New York, and at one time she had tried to divert suspicion from herself by informing on other drug dealers to the Bureau of Narcotics.

Canadian officials accompanying Benjamin made sure that no criminal activity could be proved against Vivienne at that time. Then they turned her over to two Royal Canadian Mounted Police, who were to see that she was escorted back into the United States.

But Vivienne, always ready for a party, convinced the two Mounties that they should give her a tour of Expo 67 before deporting her, and the group ended up sharing a lavish and convivial dinner. In the spirit of better Canadian-United States relations, Vivienne invited the Mounties to visit her in New York, promising to show them a really good time. Two months later they took her up on the invitation.

During the Mounties' visit to New York, Vivienne told them that she would buy any drugs they could get their hands on. One of the men had brought along an ounce of heroin stolen from the police chemist who analyzed confiscated drugs, and the Nagelbergs paid him $500 for it.

The two Mounties returned to Canada excited by their success at heroin smuggling. They then stole six kilos of confiscated heroin from a cache in the R.C.M.P. headquarters and replaced the loss with flour. At that point one of the men backed out of the deal; the other, Roger Mourant, drove to New York and sold the heroin to the Nagelbergs for $27,500 in cash. Soon after Mourant returned to Montreal the second Mountie demanded a share of the money. When Mourant turned him down, the irate Mountie reported Mourant's activities to the staff sergeant of the R.C.M.P.'s Montreal division. After Mourant had been sentenced, Assistant United States Attorney Andrew Maloney flew to Canada and managed to persuade him to testify against the Nagelbergs. Mourant's testimony ultimately put Vivienne out of circulation, but other dealers quickly moved in to supply her customers with heroin.

The road that heroin follows from the poppy fields to the addict on the streets of New York is an exotic and devious one. Turkish poppy farms supply much of the drug that comes into the United States. After the flowers have bloomed and the petals have fallen, the pods harden on the stems. The farmer makes an incision in each pod, allowing a milky juice to ooze out. As it dries, the juice turns brown and gummy. The farmer scrapes off this gum and rolls it into balls of several pounds weight, which he then sells. Whatever he can hold back from government purchasers he sells at a higher price to black market operators, who boil the balls of poppy gum with calcium chloride to obtain a less bulky substance called morphine base. They smuggle the morphine base to gangster-run laboratories in Europe, particularly in Marseilles, France.

The laboratories refine the morphine base into pure heroin (a white powder ten times more potent than morphine), which is then smuggled into the United States either directly or by way of Canada, Mexico, or South America. The importers in France let the United States importers know how much heroin is available (for about $3,500 a kilo). The buyers then place orders, but they deposit only half the money in the sellers' accounts so the sellers will share the loss if the heroin is discovered during shipping. The orders are placed either in the United States or Canada through front men, who are given a share of the profits by the racketeers. (Narcotics from the Far East are generally handled by independents rather than by organized crime groups.)

Deals are always made for lots of less than fifty kilos (110 pounds) because larger shipments would be too hard to handle. Once a shipment arrives in the United States it is usually divided four or five ways and sold to subcontractors for $15,000 to $25,000 a kilo. The subcontractors then sell to wholesalers for an equally handsome profit; the wholesalers cut it, package it, and sell it to pushers, who sell it to the addicts.

As long as addicts are desperate enough to pay the incredibly high black market prices to support their habits, the complicated machinery that moves drugs from the Middle East to the streets of America will stay well oiled. And as long as illegal drugs go on yielding millions of dollars of profit, it is certain that the bosses of organized crime will continue to cut themselves the largest piece of the pie.

10

ORGANIZED CRIME
IN THE
SUPERMARKET

To MOST PEOPLE organized crime may seem a distant danger that threatens only the corrupt, the poor, and the wayward. In fact many Americans who live in comfortable homes, shop in neighborhood supermarkets, and send their children to modern, well-equipped schools are victims of organized crime without knowing it.

Organized crime has become a big business in the United States—perhaps the biggest.* In recent years it has branched out from strictly illegal affairs like gambling, prostitution, hijacking, and loan-sharking into legitimate business. Gangsters now have invested in everything from diaper services and dress boutiques to garbage hauling companies and meat packing plants. Unfortunately, the new businessmen do not hesitate to use the methods they found so effective in the underworld to obtain high sales, new customers, and perhaps a monopoly for their businesses. The ultimate victim is always the consumer. Without suspecting it, he is the one who pays higher prices for inferior goods and services.

One way mobsters victimize consumers is by selling them spoiled foods and dangerous products, perhaps even under a respected brand name. The Merkel Meat Company of New York, for example, had an excellent reputation for years. Then the Merkel family sold the company to a man named Norman Lokietz. Under the Merkel name, he began to sell frankfurters and other ground meat products made from ingredients never intended for human consumption. Some of the main ingredients were the carcasses of diseased cows, horses, and sheep. This tainted meat was intended only as feed for minks on mink ranches, but instead it was purchased by a meat processor on Manhattan's west side, the Triangle Meat Brokers. The head of Triangle was Charles Anselmo, a loan shark associated with organized crime.

Anselmo sold the tainted meat to the Merkel plant, which turned it into frankfurters. When law enforcement officials traced the meat to the

Merkel Meat Company, they discovered that the new boss, Norman Lokietz, had "convinced" a group of inspectors from the Department of Agriculture to certify that the frankfurters met proper standards.

These deplorable practices by a company that once had the wholehearted confidence of thousands of housewives were investigated by the office of Manhattan District Attorney Frank S. Hogan and dramatized by the New York State Commission of Investigation at public hearings in 1969. The commission pointed out that gangsters had been infiltrating the meat industry since World War II, when they discovered a profit in black market meats and stolen ration stamps.

The commission said that some companies like to hire gangsters, many of whom have connections with labor unions, in the hope of buying labor peace. But it emphasized that such companies buy only trouble for themselves and ultimately for consumers.

The commission revealed what had happened when a meat company hired gangster John Dioguardi, better known as Johnny Dio, as a salesman. Johnny Dio, a captain in the Thomas Luchese Mafia family, had very impressive connections, including many with powerful labor leaders such as officials in the Teamsters Union. It was not long before Dio became the most powerful man in the company, and when that happened, the quality of the products plummeted.

According to a route salesman who delivered the company's meat to the supermarkets, it was "light in color, sometimes green, and at all times sweaty." It is standard procedure that a route salesman will take back meat if his customers, the supermarkets, are not satisfied with it, but this man's company announced to all their route salesmen that they would take no returns at all. The salesman said he felt that the meat was "an atrocity to perpetrate on our customers."

In its report on this case, the commission concluded, "The ultimate loser here, as always, was the consumer, for this policy of no returns had to mean that the retail outlets were forced to pass on this 'green, sweaty meat' to the housewife."

Not all supermarket managers, of course, knuckle under to intimidation by gangsters and agree to stock an inferior product in their stores. But then some of these managers have paid for their resistance with their lives.

Some time ago, Jerry Catena, a leading New Jersey Mafia figure, and his brother Gene went into the detergent business. They got a contract from the manufacturer of a little-known brand of detergent to sell the product to retailers in the New Jersey area. The Catena brothers already had a company called Best Sales Company of Newark, which pushed certain products on supermarkets. Their "salesmen" were the six hundred members of Jerry's gang, aided by certain members of the Amalgamated Meat Cutters and Butcher Workmen and of the Teamsters Union.

The detergent proved to be a fast mover. First the Catenas had representatives of the butchers' union mention in the supermarkets that the detergent was being sold by "particular friends of ours." Most store managers quickly took the hint and ordered an ample supply, which they priced, as directed, at 70 cents a box.

Then the Catenas decided to "persuade" the A&P chain to stock their detergent and perhaps even to give it a special push over the established brands. A&P agreed to test the detergent, but soon reported that it did not measure up to their standards and that they would not buy it.

Gene Catena became very angry and vowed to "knock A&P's brains out." First a fire bomb burned a Yonkers, New York, A&P to the ground. Then, a month later, an A&P store in Peekskill, New York, was hit with a Molotov cocktail and caught fire. Two months after that a Manhattan A&P was demolished by fire. Then a Bronx store went up in smoke.

The executives of the A&P were frightened, but they had no idea that the fires were connected with the detergent. The Catenas moved on to less subtle methods. In January of 1965 the manager of a Brooklyn A&P, driving home from his store, got a "flat tire." When he got out to fix it, four men pulled up in a car and shot him to death. Two weeks later an A&P manager from Elmont, New York, was shot and killed in his driveway. And two months after that, a fire bomb demolished another A&P store in the Bronx.

Frantic A&P officials asked the federal government to help them. Soon the government's informants in the underworld discovered that the murders and burnings could be traced back to the rejection of the detergent. The informants, however, could not produce evidence in court to prove the charge. Jerry Catena himself was brought before a federal grand jury for questioning and the campaign of terror abruptly ended. But because the government could not reveal its informants the jury returned no indictments, and no one was ever punished for the two murders and five burned-out supermarkets.

Gangsters have found that trucking products from wholesalers to retailers can be a very profitable business. Moreover their trucking firms have one great advantage over legitimate ones: their trucks are most unlikely to be hijacked. But whenever a manufacturer hires a trucker backed by criminals, one thing is certain—the service will cost more and the premium will eventually be passed on to the consumer.

Consumers were the ultimate victims several

years ago when a nationally known manufacturer of medium-priced dresses and sportswear began having difficulty getting his clothes to the stores across the country that sold them. The manufacturer's troubles started when the late Thomas "Three-Fingers Brown" Luchese, then the leader of one of the major Mafia families, paid him a visit and suggested that he give his trucking business to a firm owned by one of Luchese's relatives. The manufacturer replied that he was perfectly happy with the trucking firm he was using. Luchese smiled and left.

A few days later the first of a series of trucks carrying the garment maker's products was hijacked. Other trucks had their tires slashed or their motors damaged and were unable to make deliveries on schedule.

At first the garment maker stood firm, but when his customers complained that they had never received the clothes they had ordered or were receiving them late, his entire business was in jeopardy. So, in the end, he switched to the trucking firm run by Luchese's relative. The manufacturer's shipping troubles suddenly stopped, but just as suddenly his trucking costs rose 10 per cent in most cases. The higher trucking costs, of course, had to be passed on to the women throughout the country who bought his dresses and sportswear.

Sometimes even the vague threat of gangland connections may be enough to frighten businessmen into using underworld trucking services, as a recent article in *The Wall Street Journal* demonstrated. The *Journal* explained that most bananas imported into the United States are sold from the ships to middlemen, called jobbers. The jobbers wait until the green bananas ripen and then sell them to the retail stores. They must hire truckers to get the bananas from the docks to the fruit stores and supermarkets.

In New York and New Jersey, when the ships of three major banana importers tie up at Port Newark, New Jersey, and Pier 13 on New York's East River, the jobbers are waiting to buy. But they already know whom they will hire to haul the bananas: Ross Trucking Company. If a jobber does not promise to hire Ross Trucking Company, the three banana importers will not sell him any bananas. (The fourth and largest banana importer in the country, United Fruit Company, uses different docks and allows competing trucking companies to unload its ships.)

No one knows exactly why Ross Trucking Company is favored by the banana importers, but many believe that it has to do with the fact that the company's highest paid employee is connected with the Mafia. The Executive Director of the Waterfront Commission of New York Harbor says that Ross Trucking Company charges "exorbitant rates" and that its trucks are not insulated to protect the fruit.

Most of the jobbers are not happy about the situation, but they do not want to talk about it either. One jobber, when asked about Ross Trucking, said nervously, "Leave me out. This is strictly a cement overcoat situation." Another said, "Look, I don't question the system." But a third jobber complained, "It costs me twenty-two and a half cents a box of bananas if Ross delivers. I could save ten cents a box by sending my own truck down to the dock. But no, I'm forced to use Ross."

And if the jobber has to pay more, and if bananas are damaged in transit, consumers pay the extra cost.

Perhaps the most insidious kind of criminal infiltration into legitimate business occurs when gangster-backed companies win contracts to perform such municipal services as building schools and highways or providing the city with trucks and automobiles. Sooner or later the citizens of the town will discover that they have been saddled with outrageously expensive and dangerously unsound buildings or highways or vehicles. Mount Vernon, New York, for example, is a residential community of seventy-three thousand, but the price it pays to have its garbage hauled every year—over $200,000—was big enough to attract gangsters. In 1969 a number of homeowners complained that their garbage was frequently not collected. And the mayor of Mount Vernon suspected that on occasion truckloads of garbage had been "watered down" to increase their weight.

When inquiries were made, it was discovered that the man whose company had been awarded the contract to haul Mount Vernon's garbage had, several years previously, without the city's permission, sold his equipment and turned over the business to the Columbus Lease Corporation of Mount Vernon. It was also discovered that the Columbus Lease Corporation was run by Joseph Gambino, the thirty-nine-year-old brother of aging Mafia chieftain Carlo Gambino and a lieutenant in his Mafia family. Eventually Mount Vernon's Common Council voted to have the garbage hauled by city employees.

Communities like Mount Vernon, which are close to big cities with high crime rates, are not the only ones susceptible to pressure by the mob. No community is as removed from big cities or big-city pressures as Muskogee, Oklahoma, but the underworld apparently had no trouble reaching it.

Muskogee, a town of thirty-seven thousand, was portrayed in the top country music song of 1970 as the model city of the American "silent majority," where drugs, hippies, and draft card burnings are unknown. In that year Muskogee got a new city manager, Leonard Briley, and a new police chief, George Kennedy, thirty-two. Two previous police chiefs had quit after one had had his automobile bombed and the other had had his home fired upon after they tried to move against rackets that were controlled by "underworld elements" in the town.

Some of the fifty-two men in the city police department rebelled against the discipline imposed by their new chief. With the backing of the new city manager, Kennedy dismissed or suspended nine policemen. In October, 1970, wives of policemen began picketing City Hall to demand the ouster of Briley and Kennedy. In November, Briley said that "an underworld element" might have been stirring up trouble within the police department.

On December 10 Kennedy announced that he had learned of a plot by underworld elements and city policemen to burn the music store belonging to a city councilman who had come out against corruption in the city. On December 30 he dismissed three more policemen, and four days later the councilman's music store was burned. The fire chief said that the $100,000 fire had been caused by arson. A few minutes before the flames enveloped the store, a police car had been seen speeding away.

The size and power of organized crime, and the extent of its infiltration into legitimate business, can make an individual feel helpless to protect himself, his family, and his community from the growing menace of the mob. Yet the individual can do a great deal. Sam Tucker, a leading gangster from Cleveland, once confessed, "We don't go where we're not wanted." Organized crime can survive only where law enforcement agencies are ineffective, where public officials are unconcerned or weak, and where citizens are indifferent or afraid. What individuals can do is to help create a climate that is hostile to organized crime and a community that is aware of its menace. Probably the best recommendations for ways to discourage organized crime are contained in the report of President Johnson's Crime Commission. Among the points raised were the following:

—That the police department of every major city should have a special intelligence unit devoted solely to investigating organized criminal activity;

—That the prosecutor's office in every major city should have enough men assigned full time to organized crime;

—That citizens' and business groups should organize permanent citizen crime commissions;

—That every newspaper in major metropolitan areas where organized crime exists should designate a highly competent reporter to write only about organized crime, the corruption it causes, and government efforts to control it.

Every citizen has a right to expect effective

law enforcement. The leaders of organized crime will understand that they are not wanted only when private citizens and public officials stand together against them.

11

ORGANIZED
CRIME
ABROAD

LIKE MANY legitimate corporations, the American organized crime syndicate for the past several years has been searching beyond United States borders for new growth opportunities. The syndicate's interest in expansion stems in part, at least, from its members feeling that their horizons in the United States are becoming a bit limited. The mob's chance to control gambling has dwindled somewhat as industrialists, led by billionaire Howard Hughes, have increasingly taken over Las Vegas casinos. Furthermore, legal lotteries and municipally controlled off-track betting operations, such as the one launched in New York in 1971, are giving gangsters competition in one of their most profitable businesses—gambling.

Even more important, a major Justice Department campaign, started by the late Robert F. Kennedy when he was Attorney General, has become increasingly effective in harassing organized crime in the United States and sending many mob leaders to jail.

Beginning in the middle 1960's, therefore, organized crime bosses began to look to Europe in general and to England in particular for possible expansion. England offered several advantages: gambling in private clubs had only been legalized in 1960 and it was growing rapidly. The monthly "handle," or volume, at one big casino, the Playboy Club of London, for example, jumped from $360,000 to $1.4 million in its first year of operation. Moreover, the British government levies only ordinary property and income taxes on the gambling clubs and their owners. Nevada, by contrast, exacts special taxes on gambling receipts realized by casinos in that state. The mob was also confident that it could get away with more in England, at least for a while, than in the United States because British authorities had little experience with organized crime.

Britain's 1960 betting and gaming act legalizing certain forms of gambling was nicknamed the vicars' emancipation because one of its principal aims was to enable churches to raise money through raffles and other games. However, the law had dramatic and unforeseen effects. Because private gaming clubs were legalized, enterprising gamblers simply began opening casinos and calling them clubs. Customers "joined" by paying a small fee at the door.

Before the British government quite realized what it had started, gambling clubs were feeding so much foreign currency, particularly dollars, into the country's shaky economy that the thought of closing them down was out of the question. By 1968 there were more than one thousand gambling clubs in England, about half of them in London, with an estimated annual turnover of $1.8 billion.

Another effect of the 1960 act was to make it legal for pubs and other establishments to install slot machines for the entertainment of their customers. This was the first aspect of the law to attract United States mobsters. For when Fidel Castro took over in Cuba and closed the Havana casinos, the slot machines there had been moved back to the United States, where they were rusting in warehouses. Consequently, Antonio "Tony Ducks" Corallo, a captain in the New York Mafia family of Thomas Luchese, was dispatched to London to try to sell the slot machines. His connections were discovered, and on his second visit he was stopped at the airport and barred from entering the country. However, on his first trip he had concluded that England had great potential for organized crime. He found that although a number of criminal gangs operated there, they had neither the financing nor the experience to organize their rackets into a powerful national network.

Unable to re-enter England himself, Corallo sent an emissary to make contact with the British gangsters and try to arrange an Anglo-American underworld entente. Corallo's immediate goal was to establish a numbers network in England similar to those operating in major United States cities.

Corallo made one mistake, however. His emissary was Herbert Itkin, a New York lawyer and an informer for the Federal Bureau of Investigation. Several years later Itkin was responsible for revealing a kickback scheme involving Corallo and James L. Marcus, a key aide to New York's mayor, John V. Lindsay. While in England for Corallo, Itkin made full reports of his activities to American officials in London. He limited his criminal contacts to underworld has-beens, not the real crime leaders in the country, and Corallo's numbers empire never came into being.

As London gambling clubs multiplied during the middle 1960's, however, organized crime leaders began to send over other representatives to see how best to take advantage of the situation. About this time Dino Cellini, Meyer Lansky's casino expert, arrived in London and soon emerged as the manager of the Colony Club, one of the posh casinos in London's West End. Cellini was ultimately barred from England by the British Home Office, and the Colony was closed down in 1968. But Lansky, as was pointed out in Chapter 3, was able to secure interests in other London casinos by using less conspicuous front men than Cellini.

Other leaders of organized crime in the United States also worked hard to carve out empires in England. A group led by Angelo Bruno, head of the Mafia in Philadelphia, flew to England in 1966. According to Scotland Yard officials, Bruno and his friends not only visited every gambling club in London but also stopped at big casinos in other British cities, such as Birmingham, Manchester, and Liverpool. The purpose of the tour, Scotland Yard said, was to determine how Mafia families not yet involved in England might take advantage of the gambling boom. The gangsters concluded that there was plenty of money to be made not only by acquiring an interest in the clubs but also by providing special services to clubs in which they had no interest.

When they returned to the United States, Bruno and his friends began providing these services, such as organizing junkets to selected English gambling clubs, supplying credit information about American gamblers to British casinos, and collecting debts owed to the clubs by Americans. Angelo Bruno went into the junket business himself through fronts, as did Pinky Panarelli, a Mafia figure in central Massachusetts, and some other men linked to organized crime.

The British government frowns on junkets in which groups of gamblers are flown in at special rates, but it tolerates them because of the dollars the junketeers spend. Besides genuine customers, the Mafia also sometimes sends "mechanics," or crooked gamblers, along on junkets to try to clean out casinos that do not subscribe to its services.

By 1968 the efforts of American organized crime to expand its operations in England were so intense that an official in the United States Embassy in London warned that "American gangsters could wind up owning this town." American organized crime has established a beachhead in England, but it has not been as successful there as its leaders had hoped. This came about for two reasons. First, late in the 1960's British authorities made the gambling industry subject to a gaming board. The board was empowered to examine the ownership, finances, and policies of gambling clubs, the prime attraction for organized crime, and to withhold licenses from clubs where irregularities were discovered. The same law that created the board gave the British Home Office the authority to regulate the gaming industry as abuses arose.

These actions cut down the number of gambling clubs and made the climate in England less attractive for the mob. The leaders of organized crime, always an inventive group, have found ways to circumvent many of the regulations, including the employment of respected Britons as front men for their operations. But the regulations have made it more difficult for American gangsters to maneuver, and their initial enthusiasm for England has been somewhat dampened.

The efficiency of British law enforcement officials is the second reason that the invasion of England by American organized crime has not been as successful as anticipated. At first British authorities were hampered by a lack of knowledge of how American organized crime works. Many of them, for instance, harbored the misconception that practically all United States gangsters are of Italian descent. Thus, in 1965 Meyer Lansky, easily one of the most powerful American underworld leaders, visited England unnoticed. The British authorities did not learn that he had been there until he had left. But a short time later a group of men—most of them with Italian names—arrived at London's Heathrow Airport and were immediately surrounded by immigration officials, who held them for several hours until they discovered that the men were carpenters sent to do some repair work on the United States Embassy.

After a few such blunders, British authorities learned fast about organized crime from American law enforcement agents dispatched to London for that purpose. Within a short time Scotland Yard officials had achieved enough expertise to foil some extremely sophisticated criminal projects. In 1966, for example, the Mafia sent a man to London to develop links with local gangsters. He sought out the leaders of one of the most powerful gangs in England—men so imaginative that they are said to have contemplated kidnapping the Pope. The Mafia evidently intended to make the British gang the nucleus of an organization that would eventually direct all the rackets in Great Britain.

What the British gang needed most for such an operation was money, and the Mafia representative showed its leaders how they could make a lot of it quickly by handling securities stolen in Canada and the United States. The British gang even set up its own bank to receive the securities, stamp them to make them look legitimate, then send them to agents in Europe, who used them as collateral for big loans.

The racket worked well for some time, but British police finally uncovered it and were able to trace it back to the Mafia in the United States.

In the London hotel room of the Mafia's agent they found $90,000 worth of negotiable bonds stolen from an eminent New York law firm. A police search of the Mafia man's New York City apartment, which was made at the request of British authorities, revealed a code book used in sending cables to the English gang and its associates on the Continent.

"This case demonstrates just how far organized crime forces are willing to go to get firmly established in England," says an FBI agent who has followed the mob's international operations for years. "They've had some setbacks, but they're going to keep trying. There is a lot of money to be made over there, and they're not going to pass it up."

12

HIGH ROLLERS
ON HIGH

As THE EL AL chartered jet rose through the clouds over Kennedy Airport, the garment manufacturer from New York leaned back in his seat and dreamed of the easy money waiting for him thirty-five hundred miles away.

"I got a feeling," he said to the salesman sitting next to him, "that I'm going to come back at least five grand ahead. Maybe more. I got this thing about hunches, and I can feel it."

"I don't care if I even drop a few hundred," the salesman said. "I don't see how I can lose on this deal."

Both men were in for an expensive education, and so were most of their 130 fellow passengers on this one-week gambling junket to London. The group included engineers and doctors, wives and secretaries, industrialists and merchants, an assistant district attorney from Brooklyn, two operators of mod men's shops in Toronto, a few men who stared into space and said nothing when asked where they were from and what they did—and this writer, posing as a rich Greek shipowner.

In their gambling inclinations the junketeers ranged from big-betting high rollers to timid penny-ante types. Several had been told about the junket by friends who had taken similar trips, and a number were regular gamblers who frequently take junkets. Many were on their first such trip and did not really know what to expect. Although only proof of a healthy bank account is required to qualify, junket operators prefer applicants who have established credit at some casino. This is an indication that they are serious gamblers likely to wager sizable sums.

Each man on the plane had paid $1,000 for himself and $300 for his wife or girl friend if he had brought one along. In return, he had been promised not only a round trip flight to London, accommodations at a new hotel for a week, and a free dinner every night in the restaurant of the host casino—the Victoria Sporting Club—but also his full $1,000 back in chips to gamble with at the casino.

"If we're careful not to lose too much," said a hopeful New Jersey housewife to her husband as the plane pushed on over the Atlantic, "it will be like getting a free trip to London, won't it?"

"And we might win," said her husband, reflecting the general mood of holiday optimism among the junketeers.

The junket was organized by Eastern Sportsmen's Club, Incorporated, a New York-based company that deals in gambling tours. Eastern recruited about one hundred of the passengers, and a second concern, Wonderama Tours, brought together the rest. Two of the three partners who run Eastern—Henry Shapiro and Harold Halpern—came along on the junket, as did two representatives of Wonderama, Ted Linker and David Mitterman.

Eastern is one of the busiest junket-organizing firms on the East Coast. Once limited chiefly to Las Vegas, gambling junkets have gained great popularity in the last decade and are now run to almost every gambling center in the world from Beirut to Curaçao. An estimated one hundred thousand persons take gambling junkets from the United States every year.

By far the most popular junket destination outside Las Vegas is London, partly because of its swinging reputation and partly because there are more gambling establishments in London—they currently number about three hundred—than in practically any other city in the world.

Gambling tours themselves are perfectly legal, though some of the individuals involved with them have run afoul of the law for other activities. Eastern's Messrs. Shapiro and Halpern were indicted for renting a ship in 1966 and turning it into a floating casino after it sailed from New York on what was billed as a "cruise to nowhere." They are charged with crime on the high seas under a little-known law that forbids United States citizens from setting up shipboard gambling, even in international waters.

Some other junket organizers are known to be members or close associates of the Mafia. Many junket organizers, however, are simply legitimate travel agents.

But these matters were far from the thoughts of most of those in our tour group when our plane landed at Heathrow Airport in London on a Saturday afternoon. We were met by several attractive young women from the Victoria Sporting Club, who greeted us warmly and passed out little envelopes that, one of the girls said, contained our "keys to fun and fortune." In the envelopes were some words of welcome, tickets for free meals at the casino restaurant, and membership cards to the club. In Britian gambling is legal only at "private" clubs, but anybody can join for a small fee.

A bus then took us to the Royal Lancaster Hotel, near Hyde Park. There we had the first hint that the week might not be as ideal as envisioned by the most optimistic members of the group. Somehow the hotel did not have as many single rooms available as the sponsors of the junket had ordered, and several junketeers had to share rooms or pay extra for double-sized rooms. I took the latter choice and paid an extra $35 for the week.

A few members of the group wanted to rush to the casino right away, but they were advised by more experienced hands to rest from the flight first. "A tired gambler is a bad gambler," said a Connecticut man who had been on three previous junkets. "Besides, there won't be anything going on now. You can wait until nine, ten o'clock and still catch all the real action."

By six thirty, however, junketeers began coming down from their rooms, suitcase creases still visible on their clothes, their faces aglow with anticipation. A Rolls Royce provided by the Victoria began ferrying them to the casino. Soon there was a line for the Rolls, and the majority impatiently hailed cabs.

The Victoria Sporting Club does not look like a gambling palace from the outside. The inconspicuous entrance is on the ground floor of a modern apartment building on Edgware Road. Members show their cards and check their coats, then mount a mirrored staircase to the immense gaming room, which runs half the length of the second floor. Red velvet draperies and red carpets set off the green of the blackjack, roulette, baccarat, and craps tables. One wall of discreetly curtained windows runs the length of the gaming room, giving a faint sense of the transition from day to night—unlike the windowless, clockless casinos in Las Vegas, where it is nighttime all day long.

At the entrance to the gaming room, as we walked in, a handful of gamblers' wives waited their turn to ply the two slot machines with sixpences. Inside the room male dealers in shirtsleeves and pretty young girl dealers in lace blouses and black skirts, all looking rather bored, dealt blackjack to tables crowded with gamblers. Girls in black miniskirts, their heads piled high with hair pieces, served soft drinks (alcoholic beverages are not allowed at gambling tables in Britain) and emptied ashtrays.

Lamps with fringed shades hung over every table, supplementing the recessed lighting in the ceiling and lending a hint of gentlemen's-club atmosphere to the casino. But the droning of the croupiers, the American-accented chatter of the gamblers, and the shouts of the men at the craps table dispelled any air of elegance. In the back of the room, raised slightly above the gaming floor, was a large restaurant and bar where waiters in black rushed about, talking in Spanish, Italian, and French, and where unattached girls sat waiting for lonely gamblers to join them.

Upon arriving at the club, each member of our tour was given his $1,000 worth of chips. Those who had not been on a junket before were surprised, however, to discover that what they received were not real chips. They were markers, different in color and texture from the negotiable chips at the gaming tables. The markers could not be exchanged for cash; they could be turned into negotiable chips only by getting into a game, using the markers to place bets, and winning. The croupiers would then pay off with chips that could be exchanged for cash. Asked to make change for markers, the croupiers would simply change them with more markers.

"It's sad to watch some of these chaps," a veteran British gambler told me later. "They start off betting big with markers, hoping to convert them quickly and get out. But they usually wind up losing all of them. So they continue playing to get back their thousand, only to lose thousands more."

But no one was thinking about losing that first night at the casino, and each man moved to a table as soon as he picked up his markers. Those of little daring or experience drifted to the roulette tables, and the slightly more adventurous chose blackjack. But the high rollers went straight to the craps table. I went to a blackjack stand near the craps table, hoping to cover two fronts at once.

By 10 P.M. I was down £50 ($120) in markers, but it was clear from the shouts that echoed through the club that my friends at the craps table were doing well. A quick check revealed that the garment manufacturer was one-third of the way to the $5,000 he felt sure he was going to win, the assistant district attorney was up "a few hundred," and almost everyone else was also ahead.

Feeling that a good dinner might improve my playing, I proceeded to the casino restaurant. We had been told that we could order anything we wished, but as it turned out, that did not necessarily mean we would get what we ordered.

The first night, for example, I ordered a bottle of Chateau Yquem 1961, a sweet white wine that was, at 100 shillings ($12), one of the most expensive listed. The waiter went to get the bottle, but he was stopped a few steps from my table by a captain who instructed him in French to tell me that they were out of it.

I let the incident pass, thinking that maybe they really were out of the wine, and I returned to the blackjack table, where I lost another £100 ($240). I left for the hotel about 1 A.M., leaving the gamblers at the craps table still going strong, and judging from their jubilant shouts, still winning. The following afternoon I learned that almost everyone had finished the evening well ahead, including the garment man, who left the casino about 4 A.M. some $2,200 to the good.

On Sunday night I went directly to the casino restaurant to try my luck again with the wine list. I asked for the most expensive wine on the list, a Chateau Lafite 1959, at 120 shillings ($14.40). Again when the waiter went to get it the captain, who had watched as I ordered, stopped him. This time he came over himself and informed me that the restaurant's supply of that wine had been exhausted a few days earlier.

I then ordered a bottle of the third most expensive wine on the list, a Chateau Latour 1957, at 85 shillings ($10.20).

"We are out of that as well, monsieur," he said.

Undaunted, I tried for a Chateau Cheval Blanc 1960 at 65 shillings ($7.80).

"That, too," the captain insisted.

Finally he yielded on a bottle of Chateau Loeville Lascases 1962 at 45 shillings ($5.40). But before he went to get it, he looked at me and asked sharply: "You have such wines at home, monsieur?"

"All the time," I said.

When I returned to the gaming floor, it was clear that the odds favoring the house were beginning to have an impact at the craps table. The jubilant shouts were less frequent than they had been the night before, and increasingly they alternated with deep groans. Glum faces at the roulette table told the same story, and I continued my losing trend by dropping another $120.

By Monday the hunger to gamble had begun to subside temporarily and the panic of losing had not yet started, so several of the men who had come alone turned to other pleasures. They arrived at the casino late that night, and most had at least one girl with them. Some had two, and I saw one having dinner with three.

By Wednesday night a goodly number of junketeers were getting credit from the casino and writing big checks. A businessman who sat next to me at the blackjack table said he had called his wife and asked her to put another $5,000 in their checking account. "But she was so mad I don't know if she's going to do it," he said, fuming. "She can be a real bitch when she wants to."

At this point I was down $780 of the $1,000 in markers I had started with. But then my luck changed. It started when I won a drawing for £10 ($24). The Victoria has a drawing every hour beginning around 10 P.M. During the first five hours, the prizes are small, ranging from £10 to £25. But at 3 A.M. the club holds the main drawing of the evening, and the prize is much bigger. During our week there, prizes for the main drawing ranged from £125 ($290) to £300 ($720). The whole thing is a gimmick to keep gamblers in the casino into the early hours, and it appears to work.

I also started to do much better at the blackjack

table—partly due to the kindness of a couple of dealers. After several days of dealing to me they saw that I was far from a whiz at blackjack. So they would occasionally pass me by and quickly deal to the next man when I had a hand that had a chance of winning as it stood. (Gambling is comparatively new to England, and there are relatively few of the hard, indifferent dealers and croupiers prevalent in Las Vegas.) The dealers did not help me often enough to make their pit bosses suspicious, but they did make a difference. By the end of the evening, I had won back $230 of the $780 I had lost.

The fortunes of my fellow junketeers continued to decline, however. On the way home that night I shared a cab with the garment man who had started out with such high hopes, and I asked how he was doing. "I'm down about four thousand dollars," he said sheepishly. "But I got a feeling I'm going to get most of it back tomorrow night."

At noon Thursday I called the room of a man I had gotten to know on the flight over. "I'm not doing as bad as most," he said when I inquired, "but I feel terrible. We've been bringing these broads back with us from the casino almost every night, and I haven't had four hours sleep in the last three days. Some guys haven't slept at all. I don't see how they're able to stand up."

My friend also informed me that the group

would not be leaving on Friday as scheduled but would stay a day longer because the airline could not provide a plane in time. I thought this would be welcome news to the junketeers—a free extra day in London. But I was wrong. "They can't do this to me," an engineer from New York City said in the hotel lobby when I told him the news. "If I stay one more day, I'll be hocking my kid's bicycle when I get back. I can't win and I can't stay away from the tables. It's sadistic what they're doing."

On Thursday night I went back to the club, and at first I continued to win. But the cards turned just as I began to increase the size of my bets, and not even my friendly dealers could help me. By 11 P.M. Friday I had lost all of the $1,000 I had started with, and I spent the rest of the evening wandering around the tables to see how everyone else was doing.

Most were doing so badly they did not want to be asked where they stood. "What are you, an informer for Internal Revenue or something?" one man snapped. "Tell them in my case they got nothing to worry about. I'm losing my shirt. Does that make you happy?"

Before quitting for the night, I asked a pit boss whom I had cultivated how much the casino had made from the people on our junket. "We don't know exactly yet," he said, "but it would be about three hundred and fifty thousand dollars."

On Saturday everyone gathered in the hotel lobby for the long ride home. I had to stay an extra week in London, but I went down to see how they felt now that it was over.

The winners, of course, felt fine. "I had a wonderful time," said a housewife from Long Island, who had won $1,800. "Just wonderful. I can't wait to go again."

"I know how to bet, that's all," said a stockbroker who was $4,700 ahead. "A lot of people know how to play, but they don't know how to bet. I know how to bet."

Surprisingly, most losers did not feel too bad. They were busy practicing the fine art of rationalization.

"I was just too tired and couldn't concentrate," a merchant, down $4,600, explained. "I'm going again, but this time I'm going to take my wife along. A whole week of playing around with the girls here is too much."

"See that fellow over there, the thin one in the blue suit?" asked a salesman, down $1,300. "He dropped fifteen thousand dollars. And there are several ten-thousand-dollar losers in this room. So what's thirteen hundred dollars? Peanuts, right?"

But the garment man, down $6,800, was not letting himself off that easily. "I should have locked myself in my room after the first two days and thrown the key out the window," he said. "Better still, I should have stayed home."

THE MAFIA
ESTABLISHMENT

As OF 1971 the leaders of the twenty-six Mafia families that operate in twenty-one metropolitan areas in the United States are the following, according to reports of the Department of Justice:

NEW YORK CITY

(Five Families)

The Profaci Family
Boss—Joseph Colombo, Sr.

Underboss—Salvatore Mineo
Consigliere—Joseph Yacovelli

The Bonanno Family
Boss—Natale Evola
Underboss—Philip Rastelli
Consigliere—Joseph De Filippi

The Genovese Family
Boss—Gerardo Catena, acting boss since the death of Vito Genovese in 1969
Underboss—Thomas Eboli
Consigliere—Michele Miranda

The Gambino Family
Boss—Carlo Gambino
Underboss—Aniello Dellacroce
Consigliere—Joseph Riccobono

The Luchese Family
Boss—Carmine Tramunti
Underboss—Stefano La Salle
Consigliere—Vincent Rao

BOSTON

Boss—Raymond Patriarca
Underboss—Gennaro Angiulo
Consigliere—Joseph Lombardo

BUFFALO

Boss—Stefano Magaddino
Underboss—Joseph Fino
Consigliere—Vincent Scro

CHICAGO

Bosses—Anthony Accardo and Paul Delucia,
acting bosses due to the flight of
family boss Sam Giancana to Mexico
Underboss—John Cerone
Consigliere—Felix Alderisio

DETROIT

Boss—Joseph Zerilli
Underboss—John Priziola
Consiglieri—Angelo Meli, Peter Licavoli,
and Joseph Massei

LOS ANGELES

Boss—Nicolo Licata
Underboss—Joseph Dippolito
Consigliere—Tommy Palermo

PHILADELPHIA

Boss—Angelo Bruno Annaloro

Underboss—Ignazio Denano
Consigliere—Joseph Rugnetta

NEW JERSEY

Boss—Simone Rizzo DeCavalcante
Underbosses—Frank Majuri and
Joseph Le Salva

SAN FRANCISCO

Boss—Anthony Lima
Underboss—Gaspare Sciortino

SAN JOSE, CALIFORNIA

Boss—Joseph Cerrito
Consigliere—Steve Zoccoli

NEW ORLEANS

Boss—Carlos Marcello
Underboss—Joseph Marcello, Jr.

MIAMI

Boss—Louis Santo Trafficante, Jr.
Underboss—Stefano A. Randazzo

CLEVELAND

Boss—John Scalish

DENVER

Boss—Joseph Spinuzzi

ERIE, PENNSYLVANIA

Boss—Russell Bufalino

MILWAUKEE

Boss—Frank Balistrieri

KANSAS CITY

Boss—Nicholas Civella

PITTSBURGH

Boss—Sebastian John LaRocca

ST. LOUIS

Boss—Anthony Giordano

MADISON, WISCONSIN

Boss—Carlo Caputo

SPRINGFIELD, ILLINOIS

Boss—Frank Zito

ROCKFORD, ILLINOIS

Boss—Joseph Zammuto

INDEX

The electrifying bestseller about an American millionaire who emerges as a top Nazi!

THE SCARLATTI INHERITANCE

ROBERT LUDLUM

October, 1944

In Europe, the Third Reich is in its death struggle. In Washington, word is received that an elite member of the Nazi High Command, Heinrich Kroeger, is willing to defect and divulge information that will shorten the war. He will deal only with an obscure major in Army Intelligence, Matthew Canfield. And Canfield agrees to the rendezvous only on the condition that a Top Secret State Department file is surrendered to him with its seals unbroken!

That file contains the story of the Scarlatti Inheritance. Revelation of its contents will destroy personal fortunes, reputations, even lives!

"Gripping tension, drive, suspense . . . this year's The Godfather!" **—San Francisco Chronicle**

A Dell Book $1.50

HOW MANY OF THESE DELL BESTSELLERS HAVE YOU READ?

Fiction

1. **THE NEW CENTURIONS** by Joseph Wambaugh — $1.50
2. **THE TENTH MONTH** by Laura Z. Hobson — $1.25
3. **THE SCARLATTI INHERITANCE** by Robert Ludlum — $1.50
4. **BLUE DREAMS** by William Hanley — $1.25
5. **SUMMER OF '42** by Herman Raucher — $1.25
6. **SHE'LL NEVER GET OFF THE GROUND** by Robert J. Serling — $1.25
7. **THE PLEASURES OF HELEN** by Lawrence Sanders — $1.25
8. **THE MERRY MONTH OF MAY** by James Jones — $1.25
9. **THE DEVIL'S LIEUTENANT** by M. Fagyas — $1.25
10. **SLAUGHTERHOUSE-FIVE** by Kurt Vonnegut, Jr. — 95c

Non-fiction

1. **THE SENSUOUS MAN** by "M" — $1.50
2. **THE HAPPY HOOKER** by Xaviera Hollander — $1.25
3. **THE GRANDEES** by Stephen Birmingham — $1.50
4. **THE SENSUOUS WOMAN** by "J" — $1.25
5. **I'M GLAD YOU DIDN'T TAKE IT PERSONALLY** by Jim Bouton — $1.25
6. **THE DOCTOR'S QUICK WEIGHT LOSS DIET** by Irwin Maxwell Stillman, M.D. and Samm Sinclair Baker — $1.25
7. **NICHOLAS AND ALEXANDRA** by Robert K. Massie — $1.25
8. **THE GREAT AMERICAN FOOD HOAX** by Sidney Margolius — $1.25
9. **THE DOCTOR'S QUICK INCHES-OFF DIET** by Stillman & Baker — $1.25
10. **SURROGATE WIFE** by Valerie X. Scott as told to Herbert d'H. Lee — $1.25